The Complete Collection to Preserving Food

This Book Includes:
Dehydrating, Canning and
Preserving Food for Beginners.
101 Easy Recipes to Safely Preserve
Vegetables, Fruits, Meat and Herbs
at Home

Lydia Reed

needed) before using any of the suggested remedies, techniques, or information in this book.

Table of Contents – Canning and Preserving Food for Beginners

Table of Contents – Dehydrating Food

Canning and Preserving Food for Beginners

The Complete Guide to Water Bath and Pressure Canning, Fermenting, and Preserving Food at Home with Easy Recipes

Lydia Reed

Introduction

If you have never heard of canning before, you may be curious as to what it is, and the benefits that are associated with it. Unless you are thinking it is associated with the traditional can-can dance seen in French culture, you could probably take an educated guess as to what canning is all about.

Canning is a method used to prevent the spoiling of foods by storing them in containers, or jars, which are then sealed securely and sterilized by excessive heat over a scheduled amount of time. The reason for this simplistic yet effective system is to ensure the killing of microorganisms and deter enzymes that can often contribute to the spoilage of various food items. By adding the extra step of heating the food within the sealed container, it extracts the unwanted air and creates a vacuum-like seal to protect it from outside contaminants. Both uncooked food and cooked foods can be considered for canning.

There are two techniques that could be used to successfully master the art of canning: water bath canning and pressure canning. You can decide which canning style you would like to go with, depending on the nature of the food you are attempting to preserve. Choosing the right one will ensure that you are safely obtaining the results you want and that you are sealing in that fresh taste you do not want to lose.

Another thing to take into consideration is your altitude level. We will not get into a geography lesson here and now... but the importance of knowing where you are located will help you to understand the temperature at which you should boil your cans in order to effectively kill bacteria. Here is a chart to give you a better visual:

Lastly, you have to figure out the acidity of the foods you are attempting to contain. Meats, seafood, poultry, dairy products, and all vegetables are considered to be low-acidic foods. Therefore, pressure canning should be used for them. Fruits, jams, tomatoes, pickles, sauces, vinegar and condiments are considered high-acidic foods, so water bath canning should be used for them. All of these foods are at risk of attracting Clostridium Botulinum, which is a fancy scientific word for spore-forming bacteria that increases molding and can introduce unwanted diseases into the human body. It sounds terrifying, but that is why this book is here to teach you the proper steps to avoid this bacterium. Now that we have a basic overview of canning, let's move on to the specifics of the different methods.

There is no doubt that pressure canning is not the cheapest method of food preservation. There are a lot of other preservative techniques that are cheaper and require less effort compared to pressure canning. This must have made you ask yourself why you have to choose a quite costly and technical option over cheap and mundane ones. Pressure canning, of course, requires some specialized equipment and it demands a level of attention. However, there are more reasons you need to start pressure canning. Below are some of them.

- **Pressure Canning is not as Technical as you Imagine:** The number one reason a lot to people still avoid pressure canning method of food preservation is the technicality associated with using it. While it is true that pressure canning requires a level of expertise and attention, it is not true that you cannot use it. With the instructions in this book, you will be able to use pressure canning by yourself.

- **You get the Value of its Cost:** Every penny you spend of acquiring pressure canning equipment is worth it considering the value you will get in it. Hence, you should not count pressure canning out of your options just because of money to be used to buy the specialized equipment.

- **It Saves Money:** Having established the fact that pressure canning requires buying some specialized equipment, it is important to add that buying that equipment is a good way of saving money. First, you will not need to spend extra money buying preservative acid regularly, just as you will not need to buy a fridge or a freezer.

- **It is Reliable:** This reason alone is enough to convince you to start pressure canning. Pressure canning offers guarantee and assurance of maximum effectiveness. This means that food preserved with pressure canning cannot be spoilt for a long time.

- **It is environment-friendly:** This is another reason why you need to start pressure canning. Pressure canning does not emit poisonous gas during the steaming process, hence does no harm to the environment. You, therefore, protect the environment from further damage if you choose to start pressure canning.

- **You upgrade your Culinary Skills:** Of course, everyone wants to learn new things about different aspects of life, cooking not being am exemption to that. You might have known different ways of preserving food other than pressure canning but that should not discourage you from adding to your skills. In fact, the fact that you know how to preserve food using other techniques is the more reason you need to start pressure canning.

How Does Pressure Canning Work?

Pressure canning uses steam pressure to heat canned food, raising its temperature above the normal cooking temperature level. It is important to note that pressure canning works for both low-acid and high-acid foods by alternating their pH level so that the foods remain fresh and healthy. When used to process low-acid foods, the ideal temperature level is 240°F since the foods involved do not have the natural acidity level required to prevent spoilage on their own. What pressures canning does, in this case, is to moderate the acidity level of different ingredients of the food to point needed to preserve their taste and flavor.

This implies that pressure canning provides an alternative to adding preservative acid to food to keep it for a while. When using pressure canning, the jars are left opened and little amount of water is used for steaming. Put differently, pressure canning helps kill destructive bacteria in food through high temperature boiling to prevent premature spoilage. The secret of its effectiveness is that bacteria present in food are killed are new ones are prevented from entering by sealing the can. Meanwhile, the heat generated through boiling regulates the acidity level of the canned foods for longevity.

Chapter 1: Canning Basics

Canning Method

There are two main methods of canning; water bath canning and pressure canning. The method you choose will generally depend on the type of food you are canning. Acidic foods work fine with the water bath canning technique. For others, such as vegetables and meats, you'll want to invest in that pressure canner so you can follow that technique. You'll want to use this technique when you're making relishes, jams, pickles, fruits, salsas, condiments, and vinegar.

Water Bath Canning

For water bath canning, you're basically placing your food in a jar, wiping down the rims, affixing the lid to the jar, boiling the jars, and then removing them when it's safe. Here are more detailed instructions for this canning method:

First, make sure your jars, lids, and bands work before you use them. Don't use jars that are chipped, scratched, or compromised in any way. You don't want them to break during the canning process. Wash your jars, lids, and bands in warm water with soap, and dry them. You don't have to do any excessive sterilization. As long as they are clean, you will be fine.

Heat the jars in hot water while you prepare the food. It should not be boiling water, and you don't have to cover the jars. Simply let them rest in a pot that's half-full with hot water. This will prevent the jars from breaking when you put hot food inside them.

Prepare your recipe with whatever foods you plan to can. Remove the hot jar from the water, using a jar lifter. Fill the jars with your food, using a large spoon or a funnel. Leave at least ½ an inch of space at the top of the jar. Remove any air bubbles by pressing down on the food with a spatula or spoon.

Remove any food from the rim of the jar by wiping clean with a damp cloth. Apply the band and the lid until it is tight.

Place the jars in a large pot of water, allowing the water to completely cover the jars. Heat the water until it boils. Processing time will depend on your recipe.

When it's done, remove the jars and allow them to sit at room temperature. You'll want to leave them undisturbed for at least 12 hours.

Pressure Canning

When you want to can non-acidic foods like meats, seafood, and most vegetables, uses a pressure canner. You're following the same process, but the level of heat is far more extreme in order to protect the flavor and safety. The pressurized process removes the threat of bacteria.

Foods Suitable for Pressure Canning Preservation Method

Pressure canning can be used to preserve both high-acid foods and low-acid foods. Examples of low-acid foods are:

- Banana
- Seafood
- Dairy products
- Vegetables
- Poultry
- Etc.

Examples of high-acid foods are:

- Meat
- Grains
- Legumes
- Egg
- Fish
- Beans
- Etc.

Canning Equipment

Equipment and Instructions for Operating Pressure Canning

Before diving into the instructions, let us quickly take a look at some equipment you need to begin pressure canning. The following are the basic equipment required to begin pressure canning.

- Pressure canner
- Canning jars
- Lids
- Jar lifter
- Stirrer
- Timer
- Spoon
- Mixing bowl
- Towels

Operating pressure canning requires a level of expertise and attention. And for this reason, a lot of people opt for easier alternatives which, unfortunately, cannot replace pressure canning. However, you will find operating pressure canning very easily if you follow the instructions below. Note that these operating instructions are applicable to canning all recipes of food. You should, therefore, refer back to them in addition to the specific instructions for preparing each recipe.

- Place the pressure canner on your burner.
- Insert the rack into the pressure canner.
- Pour some water into a jar and place the jar on its rack in the pressure canner.
- Then cover the canner and seal it.
- Set the burner to its highest heat level to start steaming.

- Leave the canner to steam for 10 minutes.

- Add the weight.

- Wait for the pressure gauge to signal that it has reached the expected pressure which is usually 11 lbs.

- Then, start timing.

- At this point, you will adjust the burner's heat level to the initially expected level signaled by the pressure gauge, and process for five to fifteen minutes.

- Afterwards, switch off the burner and allow the pressure canner to cool off. Ensure you wait till the pressure is vented.

- Remove the weight, open it up and fetch the jars. Then place the jars on a cooling towel carefully and leave it for 8 to 10 hours.

Pressure Canning Safety Tips

Just like all other culinary activities, pressure canning is accompanied by different risks. Hence, you need to take some precautionary measures to help you process your foods successfully and also achieve safety. Below are some of the safety tips.

- Use the right and appropriate pressure canner in terms of size and quality.

- Use only jars that are in good shape.

- Always confirm the functionality of the gauge.

- Ensure that your pressure canner's gasket is soft and pliable always.

- Sanitation is important. Do not use any equipment except it is clean.

- Use endorsed recipes only.

- Do not over-heat or under-heat the canner.

- Stick to the processing time.

- Always allow your jars to cool naturally.

Tips for Food Safety

The whole purpose of preserving food, no matter the process, is to keep it safe for consumption at a later date. In keeping with this premise, the author advises adherence to all tips and warnings given throughout this book. Infections resulting from bacteria, fungus, or parasites can lead to anything from indigestion to death. These infections and their causes are never to be taken lightly.

According to the Center for Disease Control and Prevention (CDC), in the United States of America, roughly 48 million people are sickened each year by the foodborne pathogen. Of those, 128,000 are hospitalized, and 3,000 die. In 2011, the latest information released by the CDC, the most common illnesses were caused by Norovirus, Salmonella, and Campylobacter. Why do foodborne diseases and infections occur, and why are there so many today? These are reasonable questions asked by reasonable individuals and statehoods. The answers are both simple and complex.

Were you aware that Tuberculosis, Typhoid Fever, and Cholera were common foodborne illnesses less than a century ago? Today we have Hemolytic Uremic Syndrome in children (a type of acute kidney failure) caused by E. coli O157:H7. We also know that Guillain-Barre Syndrome an autoimmune disorder causing weakness in muscles can be caused by Campylobacter infection.

Easy transportation allows infectious agents to spread more quickly than in the past. Also, these microbes continue to evolve, changing their characteristics, and the symptoms of the illnesses they cause.

Unsafe production methods, environmental impacts, ecological factors, production practices, and even consumption habits all impact whether a microbe will find its way into our food supply.

Laboratory tests also continue to evolve, allowing the capability to recognize far more infection-causing organisms than ever before. Also, the impact of instantaneous world-wide communication should not be discounted.

As scary as this information may be, the best way to avoid causing illness for your family or yourself is common sense. In regards to food preservation, most foodborne illness can be avoided if you:

- Wash your hands thoroughly before handling food; ensure all tools and surfaces used are also clean.

- Rinse produce under running water, rubbing the entire surface with your clean hands. Soaps or detergents are not necessary; the friction of the hands loosens bacteria-holding dirt and grime, and running water washes it away.

- Don't allow product to soak. Use colanders or sieves for small foodstuffs, and make sure to keep layers shallow,

- so that all surfaces of each individual berry, bean, or other food are rinsed as thoroughly as possible.
- Never allow fluid from raw meats to touch, even with minuscule splatters, any equipment or utensil that will come in contact with fruits or vegetables, or with the fruits or vegetables themselves.
- Sanitize everything that comes in contact with raw meat or its juices.
- When preserving any foodstuffs, always use sanitary practices.
- If sterilized containers or equipment are called for, make sure to sterilize them.
- Keep raw, cooked, processed, and unprocessed foods separate at all times.

The extra steps may seem like a lot of work requiring extra time and energy; however, when compared to the time required to recover from a foodborne illness, not to mention the cost of possible hospitalization and medication, it is a minor inconvenience at worst.

Food preservation, whether by salting, sugaring, canning, or freezing is the art of killing microbes, or at least keeping them from reproducing to toxic levels.

Refrigerating or freezing food prevents bacteria from growing, preserving them in a state of suspended animation. Unfortunately, there are at least two bacteria that can grow at refrigerator temperatures. High salt, sugar, or acid levels also keep bacteria from growing.

Only heat actually kills the microbes. A temperature above 160°F [78°C], if held for even just a few seconds, is sufficient to kill parasites, viruses, and bacteria, except for one. The bacteria Clostridium produces a heat-resistant spore that can only be killed at temperatures above boiling. Pressure canning produces the temperature necessary to kill these spores.

The toxins produced by bacteria are not all affected by heat. Therefore it is very important to preserve only good quality foodstuffs. Avoid:

- Bruised fruit
- Split peels or skins
- Evidence of insect attacks
- Nibbles by birds or animals

Make sure all foodstuffs are as fresh as possible and processed in small, manageable batches as quickly as possible. Processing on the same day as harvested, and handling in a sanitary way produces the highest quality preserved foods. Again, food safety should be your paramount concern when preserving foodstuffs for future use.

Chapter 2: Water Bath Canning: Pickles

1. Pickled Green Beans

Preparation time: 20 minutes

Cooking time: 10 minutes

Servings: 4 pints

INGREDIENTS:

- 1¾ lbs. fresh green beans
- 1 tsp. cayenne pepper
- 4 garlic cloves, peeled
- 4 tsp. dill seed
- 2½ cups water
- 2½ cups white vinegar
- ¼ cup canning salt

DIRECTIONS:

1. Pack beans into four hot 1-pint jars to within ½-inch of the top.

2. Add dill seed, cayenne, and garlic to jars.

3. In a large saucepan, bring the vinegar, water, and salt to a boil.

4. Carefully scoop the hot liquid over beans, leaving ¼-inch space of the top. Remove air bubbles and if necessary, adjust headspace by adding hot mixture. Wipe the rims carefully. Place tops on jars and screw on bands until fingertip tight.

5. Place jars into canner with boiling water, ensuring that they are completely covered with water. Let boil for 10 minutes. Remove jars and cool.

NUTRITION: Carbohydrates 2g; Fat 0g; Protein 1g; Sodium: 83mg; Calories 9

2. Pickled Peppers

Preparation time: 20 minutes
Cooking time: 10 minutes
Servings: 4 pints
INGREDIENTS:

- 4 cups white vinegar
- 2 water cups
- 2 tablespoons sugar
- Olive oil
- 1 onion, medium diced
- 2 medium-sized carrots, medium diced
- Peppers
- Dried oregano
- Bay leaves

DIRECTIONS:

1. Mix together the vinegar, water, and sugar in a medium saucepan and heat until the mixture reaches a simmer.

2. Meanwhile, sauté the onions and carrots in olive oil until tender.

3. Using pint-sized canning jars, place approximately 1 tablespoon of the mixture in the bottom of a jar, then add the peppers (if you make 3 small incisions on each pepper, the flavors of the brine will infuse more quickly).

4. Add one bay leaf and 1/2 teaspoon of oregano to each jar. Seal the jars, and process in a hot water bath for 10 minutes.

5. The flavor for these peppers will be best after at least two weeks.

Nutrition: Carbohydrates 17.59g; Fat 1.7g; Protein 1.15g; Sodium 50mg; Calories – 140

3. Pickled Beets

Preparation time: 85 minutes

Cooking time: 35 minutes

Servings: 4 pints

INGREDIENTS:

- 3 lbs. fresh, small beets
- 2 sugar cups
- 2 water cups
- 2 cider vinegar cups
- 2 cinnamon sticks
- 1 tsp. whole cloves
- 1 tsp. whole allspice

DIRECTIONS:

1. Scrub beets and detruncate tops to 1 inch. Put in a Dutch oven and cover with water. Bring to a boil.

2. Reduce heat and let simmer, covered, until tender, 25-35 minutes.

3. Remove from water and let cool. Peel beets and cut into fourths.

4. Place beets in a Dutch oven with vinegar, sugar, and water.

5. Wrap cinnamon sticks, cloves, and allspice in a double thickness of cheesecloth. Add to beet mixture.

6. Bring to a boil, then reduce heat and cover. Let simmer 10 minutes. Discard spice bag.

7. Pack beets into four hot sterilized 1-pint jars to within ½-inch of the top.

8. Carefully scoop the hot liquid over beets, leaving ¼-inch space of the top. Remove air bubbles and if necessary, adjust headspace by adding hot mixture. Wipe the rims carefully. Place tops on jars and screw on bands until fingertip tight.

9. Place jars into canner with boiling water, ensuring that they are completely covered with water. Let boil for 35 minutes. Remove jars and cool.

NUTRITION: Carbohydrates 12g; Fat 0g; Protein 1g; Sodium 44mg; Calories 53

4. Chunky Zucchini Pickles

Preparation time: 85 minutes

Cooking time: 35 minutes

Servings: 4 pints

INGREDIENTS:

- 14 cups seeded, unpeeled zucchini (I peeled half of them because this zucchini was huge and the skin was tougher than smaller zucchini)
- 6 cups finely chopped onions
- 1/4 cup pickling or canning salt
- 3 cups granulated sugar
- 4 tbsp. Clearjel (I have never seen this in stores but you can purchase it online ~ I used 2 tbsp. of corn starch)
- 1/4 cup dry mustard
- 1 tbsp. ground ginger
- 1 tsp. ground turmeric
- 1/2 cup water
- 2 cups white vinegar
- 1 red bell pepper, seeded and finely chopped

DIRECTIONS:

1. In a large glass or stainless steel bowl, combine zucchini and onions. Sprinkle with pickling salt, cover, and let stand at room temperature for 1 hour. Transfer to a colander placed over a sink and drain thoroughly. Note: I also rinsed half the mixture

because that is what I've done in the past with pickles…but it says DRAIN not rinse. They still seemed salty.

2. Prepare for water-bath canning. Sterilize jars in the oven on 250F for 30 minutes.

3. In a large stainless steel saucepan, combine sugar, Clearjel or corn starch, mustard, ginger, and turmeric. Stir dry ingredients well. Gradually blend in water. Add vinegar and red pepper.

4. Bring to a boil over medium-high heat, stirring frequently to dissolve sugar and prevent lumps from forming. Reduce heat and boil gently, stirring frequently, until mixture thickens about 5 minutes. Add drained zucchini mixture and return to a boil.

5. Ladle hot zucchini mixture into hot sterilized jars, leaving 1/2" headspace. Remove air bubbles and adjust headspace, if necessary, by adding more hot zucchini mixture. Wipe rim with a damp paper towel. Place snaps and rings on each jar, screwing bands down until they are fingertip-tight.

6. Place jars in canner, ensuring they are completely covered with water. Bring to a full rolling boil and process for 10 minutes. When time is up, turn off the heat, remove canner lid and wait 5 minutes before removing jars to a folded towel on the counter.

7. Check seals, label, and store. Refrigerate any unsealed jars.

NUTRITION: Carbohydrates 154.14g; Fat 3.47g; Protein 11.58g; Sodium 395mg; Calories 683

5. Pickled Brussels Sprouts

Preparation time: 30 minutes

Cooking time: 10 minutes

Servings: 6 pints

INGREDIENTS:

- 3 lbs. fresh Brussels sprouts halved
- 1 medium sweet red pepper, finely chopped
- 6 garlic cloves, halved
- 1 medium onion, thinly sliced
- 2 tsp. crushed red pepper flakes
- 1 tbsp. celery seed
- 1 tbsp. whole peppercorns
- 3 tbsp. canning salt
- ½ sugar cup

- 2½ white vinegar cups
- 2½ water cups

DIRECTIONS:

1. Fill a Dutch oven three-fourths full with water; bring to a boil.
2. Add Brussels sprouts in batches, cooking, uncovered, 4 minutes until tender-crisp.
3. With a slotted spoon remove and drop into ice water. Drain and pat dry.
4. Pack Brussels sprouts into six hot 1-pint jars.
5. Divide garlic and pepper flakes among jars.
6. In a large saucepan, bring remaining ingredients to a boil.
7. Carefully scoop the hot liquid over Brussels sprouts, leaving ¼-inch space of the top. Remove air bubbles and if necessary, adjust headspace by adding hot mixture. Wipe the rims carefully. Place tops on jars and screw on bands until fingertip tight.
8. Place jars into canner with simmering water, ensuring that they are completely covered with water. Let boil for 10 minutes. Remove jars and cool.

NUTRITION: Carbohydrates 3g; Fat 0g; Protein 1g; Sodium 11mg; Calories 14

Chapter 3: Water Bath Canning: Jams, Jellies, and Preserves

6. Strawberry Jam

Preparation time: 30 minutes

Cooking time: 10 minutes

Servings: 4 pints

INGREDIENTS:

- 2 quarts of whole strawberries
- 7 cups of sugar
- ¼ cup of lemon juice
- 3 fluid ounces of liquid pectin (1 Pouch)

Directions:

1. Remove stems and caps from strawberries.
2. Wash strawberries thoroughly but quickly.
3. Press the washed strawberries through a strainer or mash with a potato masher if preferred.
4. Measure 4 cups of strawberries (crushed) into a large kettle
5. Now add the lemon juice and sugar and stir well.
6. Now bring the kettle to a vigorous boil.
7. When kettle starts to boil vigorously, leave it on the heat for 1 minute, and keep stirring. When the minute has elapsed remove kettle from the heat.
8. Now add the pectin and stir in.

9. Using a metal spoon, you will need to skim off foam.

10. Immediately fill your jars leaving ¼ inch headspace.

11. Clean jar rims, adjust lids, and heat process.

12. Process for 5 minutes at altitudes less than 1,000 feet or 10 minutes at altitudes above 1,000 feet

NUTRITION: Carbohydrates 274.56g; Fat 0.31g; Protein 1.06g; Sodium 7mg; Calories 1063

7. Raspberry Jam

Preparation Time: 5 minutes

Cooking Time: 15 minutes

Servings: 5 half-pint jars

INGREDIENTS:

- 4 cups of raspberries
- 1 package of pectin
- 2 tablespoons of lemon juice
- 3 ½ cups of sugar

DIRECTIONS:

1. Crush the raspberries in a large saucepan, and put on high heat. Add the lemon juice and the pectin. Bring to a boil while stirring constantly.

2. Add the sugar and mix until dissolved. Let it cook for one more minute, and then remove from heat.

3. Pour the jams into the jars equally, cover, and let the jars sit in a water bath for about 10 minutes.

4. Let cool completely before storing.

NUTRITION: Carbohydrates 158.93g; Fat 0.36g; Protein 2.19g; Sodium 35mg; Calories 616

8. Blackberry Jam

Preparation Time: 5 minutes

Cooking Time: 15 minutes

Servings: 4 half-pints

INGREDIENTS:

- 4 crushed blackberries cups
- 4 sugar cups

DIRECTIONS:

1. Place the crushed blackberries into a large stockpot. Add the sugar and let rest for 1 hour. Bring to a boil over medium-high heat, stirring constantly, until the mixture thickens. Remove the pot from heat and skim.

2. Pour the mixture into sterile jars and adjust the lids. Process for 5 minutes in boiling water bath.

NUTRITION: Carbohydrates 211.87g; Fat 0.48g; Protein 4.47g; Sodium 13mg; Calories 833

9. Plum Orange Jam

Preparation time: 30 minutes

Cooking time: 5 minutes

Servings: 10 half-pints

INGREDIENTS:

- 10 cups chopped plums, skinless
- 1 cup of orange juice
- 1 package pectin
- 3 sugar cups
- 3 tbsp. grated orange zest
- 1½ tsp. ground cinnamon

DIRECTIONS:

1. In a Dutch oven, combine orange juice and plums and bring to boil.

2. Reduce heat and simmer, covered, 5-7 minutes or until softened, stirring occasionally.

3. Stir in pectin. Bring to a rolling boil, stirring constantly.

4. Stir in cinnamon, sugar, and orange zest. Let boil for 1 minute, stirring until sugar completely dissolves.

5. Remove from heat and skim off foam.

6. Scoop the hot mixture in hot sterilized half-pint jars, leaving ¼-inch space of the top. Remove air bubbles and if necessary, adjust headspace by adding hot mixture. Wipe the rims carefully. Place tops on jars and screw on bands until fingertip tight.

7. Place jars into canner with boiling water, ensuring that they are completely covered with water. Let boil for 5 minutes. Remove jars and cool.

NUTRITION: Carbohydrates 13g; Fat 0g; Protein 0g; Calories 50

10. Peach Jam

Preparation time: 30 minutes

Cooking time: 5 minutes

Servings: 8 half-pints

INGREDIENTS:

- 4 ¼ cups crushed peaches
- ¼ cup lemon juice
- 7 sugar cups
- ½ bottle liquid pectin (1.5 oz.)

DIRECTIONS:

1. Place the crushed peaches in a large pot. Add the sugar and the lemon juice and bring to a boil, stirring constantly, for 1 minute. Remove the pot from heat and stir in the pectin.
2. Pour the mixture into sterile jars and adjust the lids. Process for 5 minutes in a boiling water bath.

NUTRITION: Carbohydrates 185.1g; Fat 0.25g; Protein 1.04g; Calories 713

11. Grape Jelly

Preparation time: 30 minutes

Cooking time: 5 minutes

Servings: 4 half-pints

INGREDIENTS:

- 4 cups of prepared juice (about 3 kilos of full ripe Concord grapes)
- 7 cups (3 pounds) of sugar
- 1/2 bottle of fruit pectin

DIRECTIONS:

1. First, prepare the fruit. Root and crush about 3 kg of fully ripe grapes. Add
2. 1/2 cup of water; boil, cover for 10 minutes. Put it in the jelly cloth or bag and squeeze the juice. Measure 4 glasses in a very large pot. (If using wild grapes or other peel, use 3 1/2 cups of juice and add 1/4 cup of filtered lemon juice.)
3. To the juice measured in a pot, add the exact amount of sugar specified in the recipe. Mix well.
4. Put on high heat and boil, stirring constantly. Stir at once. Then bring it to a full boil for 1 minute, stirring constantly. Remove from the heat, filter the foam with a metal spoon, and quickly pour it into the glasses.
5. Process for 10 minutes after pouring into the sterilized jars

NUTRITION: Carbohydrates 208.37g; Fat 0.3g; Protein0.4g; Calories 820

12. Apricot Jam

Preparation Time: 15 minutes

Cooking Time: 45 minutes

Servings: 10 cups

INGREDIENTS:

- 8 cups of diced apricots, peeled and cored
- ¼ cup of lemon juice
- 6 cups of sugar

DIRECTIONS:

1. Mix all of the ingredients together in a large stock pot, and stir until the sugar is dissolved.
2. Once at a rolling boil, let it boil for about 30 minutes, then remove from heat and put into jars.
3. Let the jars sit in a water bath for about 10 minutes.
4. Let cool completely before storing.

NUTRITION: Carbohydrates 250.8g; Fat 1.9g; Protein 7.09g; Calories 971

13. Raspberry Peach Jam

Preparation time: 35 minutes

Cooking time: 15 minutes

Servings: 3 half-pints

INGREDIENTS:

- 2⅔ cups peeled, chopped peaches
- 1½ cup crushed raspberries
- 3 sugar cups
- 1½ tsp. lemon juice

DIRECTIONS:

1. In a Dutch oven, combine all ingredients.
2. Cook over medium-low heat. Stir until the sugar has dissolved and the mixture is bubbly about 10 minutes.
3. Bring to a full boil for 15 minutes, stirring constantly.

4. Remove from heat and skim off foam.

5. Carefully scoop the hot mixture into hot sterilized half-pint jars, leaving ¼-inch space of the top. Remove air bubbles. Wipe the rims carefully. Place tops on jars and screw on bands until fingertip tight.

6. Place jars into canner with boiling water, ensuring that they are completely covered with water. Let boil for 15 minutes. Remove jars and cool.

NUTRITION: Carbohydrates 8g; Fat 0g; Protein 0g; Calories 33

14. Apricot Amaretto Jam

Preparation time: 30 minutes

Cooking time: 10 minutes

Servings: 8 half-pints

INGREDIENTS:

- 4¼ cups peeled, crushed apricots
- ¼ cup lemon juice
- 6¼ cups sugar, divided
- 1 package powdered fruit pectin
- ½ teaspoon unsalted butter
- ⅓ Cup amaretto

DIRECTIONS:

1. In a Dutch oven, combine lemon juice and apricots.

2. In a small bowl, combine pectin and ¼ cup sugar. Stir into apricot mixture and add butter. Bring to a full boil over medium-high heat, stirring constantly.

3. Stir in the remaining sugar and let boil 1-2 minutes, stirring constantly.

4. Remove from heat and stir in amaretto.

5. Let the jam sit for 5 minutes, stirring occasionally.

6. Divide the hot mixture between eight hot sterilized half-pint jars, leaving ¼-inch space of the top. Wipe the rims carefully. Place tops on jars and screw on bands until fingertip tight.

7. Place jars into canner with boiling water, ensuring that they are completely covered with water. Let boil for 10 minutes. Remove jars and cool.

NUTRITION: Carbohydrates 21g; Fat 0g; Protein 0g; Calories 86

15. Blueberry Jam

Preparation Time: 20 minutes

Cooking Time: 30 minutes

Servings: 6 half-pint jars

INGREDIENTS:

- 2 pints of blueberries
- 2 tablespoons of lemon juice
- 3 ounces of pectin
- 5 ¼ cups of sugar

DIRECTIONS:

1. Combine all ingredients into a large pot and bring to a boil, stir until sugar has dissolved about 20 minutes.
2. Remove from heat and put into jars, let the jars sit in a water bath for 30 minutes.
3. Let cool completely before storing.

NUTRITION: Carbohydrates 125.6g; Fat 0.58g; Protein 1.13g; Calories 493

Chapter 4: Water Bath Canning: Salsas and Relishes

16. Corn Relish

Preparation Time: 20 minutes

Cooking Time: 50 minutes

Servings: 3-4 pints

INGREDIENTS:

- 1 large cucumber, peeled, seeded, roughly chopped
- 2 cups of chopped onions
- 1 red bell peppers, seeded and chopped
- 4 cups corn kernels (cut from 4-6 ears, depending on how big the ears are)
- 2 plum or Roma tomatoes, diced the size of a corn kernel
- 1 red or green serrano chile peppers, seeded and minced
- 1 1/4 cups sugar
- 2 tablespoons kosher salt
- 1/2 teaspoon black pepper
- 1 1/2 cups apple cider vinegar (5% acidity)

- 1/2 teaspoon turmeric
- 2 teaspoons mustard seeds
- 1/2 teaspoon ground cumin

DIRECTIONS:

1. Pulse cucumbers, onions, bell peppers: Working in batches if necessary, pulse the cucumbers, onions, and bell peppers in a food processor just 3 or 4 pulses, so they are still distinguishable from each other, not puréed.

2. Combine with remaining ingredients, simmer 25 minutes: Place mixture in a medium-sized (4 to 6-quart), thick-bottomed pot. Add the corn, tomatoes, serano chiles, sugar, salt, pepper, vinegar, turmeric, mustard seed, and ground cumin. Bring to a boil. Reduce heat to a simmer. Cover and cook for 25 minutes.

3. Scoop into jars: Spoon the corn relish into clean jars and seal, will last for 4-6 weeks refrigerated.

TIP: If you would like to store your pickles outside of the refrigerator, sterilize canning jars before canning, and process the relish-filled jars in a hot water bath for 15 minutes after canning. Review more detailed canning instructions in our recipe for bread and butter pickles.

NUTRITION: Carbohydrates 81.26g; Fat 1.98g; Protein 6.87g; Calories 354

17. Salsa Verde

Preparation Time: 20 minutes

Cooking Time: 10 minutes

Servings: 3 pints

INGREDIENTS:

- 3 glass pint jars with lids and bands
- 12 medium green tomatoes, cored, peeled and diced
- 6 to 8 jalapenos, seeded and minced
- 2 large red onions, diced
- 1 teaspoon of minced garlic
- ½ cup of fresh lime juice
- ½ cup of fresh chopped cilantro
- 1 ½ teaspoons ground cumin
- 1 teaspoon dried oregano
- Salt and pepper to taste

DIRECTIONS:

1. Prepare your water bath canner as well as your lids and bands.
2. Combine the tomatoes, jalapenos, onion, garlic, and lime juice in a large saucepan.
3. Cover and bring to a boil then stir in the remaining ingredients.
4. Reduce heat and simmer for 5 minutes then spoon the mixture into your jars, leaving about ½-inch of headspace.
5. Clean the rims add the lid and seal with a metal band then place the jars in the water bath canner and bring the water to boil.

6. Process the jars for 20 minutes then remove the jars and wipe them dry.

7. Place the jars on a canning rack and cool for 24 hours before storing it.

Nutrition: Carbohydrates 63.26g; Fat 2.27g; Protein 12.1g; Calories 276

18. Simple Salsa

Preparation Time: 20 minutes

Cooking Time: 10 minutes

Servings: 3 pints

INGREDIENTS:

- 4 cups of slicing tomatoes (peeled, cored and chopped)
- 2 cups of green chilies (seeded and chopped)
- ¾ cup of onions (chopped)
- ½ cup of jalapeno peppers (seeded and chopped)
- 4 garlic cloves (chopped finely)
- 1 teaspoon of ground cumin
- 1 tablespoon of cilantro
- 1 tablespoon of oregano
- 2 cups of distilled white vinegar
- 1 ½ teaspoon of table salt

DIRECTIONS:

1. Place all the ingredients above in a large pot. Place the pot on the stove and bring to a rolling boil while stirring constantly to prevent burning.

2. Reduce the heat a bit and let the mixture simmer for about 20 minutes. Stir frequently.

3. Divide the salsa among 4 jars. Make sure to leave about ½-inch of space at the top of each jar. Place the lids on the jars and process using the water bath canning method for 15 to 25 minutes.

NUTRITION: Carbohydrates 37.18g; Fat 9.35g; Protein 9.33g; Calories 225

19. Mango Salsa

Preparation Time: 20 minutes

Cooking Time: 10 minutes

Servings: 3 pints

INGREDIENTS:
- 1/2 water cup
- 1 ¼ cup of cider vinegar, 5%
- 2 teaspoons of ginger, chopped finely
- 1 ½ cup of red bell pepper, diced
- 1/2 teaspoon of red pepper flakes, crushed
- 6 cups of mango, unripe, diced
- 1/2 cup of yellow onion, chopped finely
- 2 teaspoons of garlic, chopped finely
- 1 cup of brown sugar, light

DIRECTIONS:
1. Thoroughly wash the mangoes and the rest of the produce.
2. Peel the mangoes before chopping in half-inch cubes.
3. Chop the yellow onion into fine bits and dice the red bell pepper in half-inch strips. Place in a stockpot or Dutch oven. Add all other ingredients, stir to combine, and heat over high heat.
4. Once the mixture is boiling, give it a good stir to dissolve the sugar. Turn the heat down to medium and allow the mixture to simmer for about five minutes.
5. Pour the hot salsa into clean and hot Mason jars, leaving half an inch of headspace in each jar. Pour the hot liquid into it to fill each jar half an inch from the rim.
6. Take out any air bubbles before securing the jar lids. Place in the pressure canner and process for ten minutes.

NUTRITION: Carbohydrates 66.93g; Fat 3.4g; Protein 2.76g; Calories 299

20. Pineapple Chipotle

Preparation Time: 20 minutes

Cooking Time: 10 minutes

Servings: 3 pints

INGREDIENTS:

- 4 Cups of seeded papaya
- 2 Cups of chopped or cubed pineapples
- 1 Cup of raisins
- 1 Cup of lemon juice
- ½ Cup of lime juice
- ½ Cup of pineapple juice
- ½ Cup of Anaheim peppers
- 2 Teaspoons of chopped onions
- 2 Teaspoons of chopped cilantro
- 2 Teaspoons of brown sugar

DIRECTIONS:

1. Add together all 10 ingredients together in a saucepan and bring to a bowl, but you need to stir constantly.
2. Reduce to a steady simmer and let thicken but still stirring constantly.
3. Add to the canning jars and seal.

NUTRITION: Carbohydrates 60.1g; Fat 0.93g; Protein 2.24g; Calories 233

21. Green Salsa

Preparation Time: 20 minutes

Cooking Time: 10 minutes

Servings: 3 pints

INGREDIENTS:

- 7 Cups of chopped green tomatoes
- 3 Cups of chopped jalapenos
- 2 Cups of chopped red onions
- 2 Teaspoons of minced garlic
- ½ Cup of lime juice
- ½ Cup of finely packed chopped cilantro
- 2 Tsp. ground cumin

DIRECTIONS:

1. Combine all the vegetables and the garlic and lime in a saucepan and boil then simmer for 5 minutes, spoon salsa into canning jars, and leave ¼" at the top for the canning process.

NUTRITION: Carbohydrates 30.31g; Fat 1.22g; Protein 5.65g; Calories 133

22. Zesty Salsa

Preparation Time: 20 minutes

Cooking Time: 10 minutes

Servings: 6 pints

INGREDIENTS:

- 10 cups roughly chopped tomatoes
- 5 cups chopped and seeded bell peppers
- 5 cups chopped onions
- 2 1/2 cups hot peppers, chopped, seeded
- 1 1/4 cups cider vinegar
- 3 garlic cloves, minced
- 2 tablespoons cilantro, minced
- 3 teaspoons salt
- 1 (6 ounces) can tomato paste

DIRECTIONS:

1. Combine all ingredients except tomato paste in a large saucepot.
2. Simmer until desired thickness.

3. Stir in tomato paste.

4. Ladle hot salsa into hot jars leaving 1/4 inch head-space.

5. Process 15 minutes in a hot water bath

6. Note: use more hot peppers for a very hot salsa or less for mild.

7. It depends on how hot your peppers are and how hot you like your salsa.

8. I never get close to 2 1/2 cups for our mild salsa.

NUTRITION: Carbohydrates 30.7g; Fat 0.86g; Protein 5.82g; Calories 142

23. Tomatillo Salsa

Preparation Time: 20 minutes

Cooking Time: 10 minutes

Servings: 2 1/2 cups

INGREDIENTS:

- 1 ½ pounds tomatillos (about 12 medium), husked and rinsed
- 1 to 2 medium jalapeños, stemmed (omit for mild salsa, use 1 jalapeño for medium salsa and 2 jalapeños for hot salsa, and note that spiciness will depend on heat of actual peppers used)
- ½ cup chopped white onion (about ½ medium onion)
- ¼ cup packed fresh cilantro leaves (more if you love cilantro)
- 2 tablespoons to ¼ cup lime juice (1 to 2 medium limes, juiced), to taste
- ½ to 1 teaspoon salt, to taste
- Optional variation: 1 to 2 diced avocados, for creamy avocado salsa verde

DIRECTIONS:

1. Preheat the broiler with a rack about 4 inches below the heat source. Place the tomatillos and jalapeño(s) on a rimmed baking sheet and broil until they're blackened in spots, about 5 minutes.

2. Remove the baking sheet from the oven, carefully flip over the tomatillos and pepper(s) with tongs, and broil for 4 to 6 more minutes, until the tomatillos are splotchy-black and blistered.

3. Meanwhile, in a food processor or blender, combine the chopped onion, cilantro, 2 tablespoons lime juice and ½ teaspoon salt. Once the tomatillos are out of the oven, carefully transfer the hot tomatillos, pepper(s) and all of their juices into the food processor or blender.

4. Pulse until the mixture is mostly smooth and no big chunks of tomatillo remain, scraping down the sides as necessary, season to taste with additional lime juice and salt if desired.

5. The salsa will be thinner at first, but will thicken up after a few hours in the refrigerator, due to the naturally occurring pectin in the tomatillos. If you'd like to make creamy avocado salsa verde, let the salsa cool down before blending in 1 to 2 diced avocados (the more avocado, the creamier it gets).

NUTRITION: Carbohydrates 37.58g; Fat 4.57g; Protein 4.32g; Calories 180

24. Corn & Cherry Tomato Salsa

Preparation Time: 20 minutes

Cooking Time: 10 minutes

Servings: 6 pints

INGREDIENTS:

- 5 pounds cherry tomatoes, roughly chopped

- 2 cups corn kernels (about 2 large ears fresh, but frozen-thawed is fine)

- 1 cup red onion, finely chopped

- 2 teaspoons salt

- ½ cup fresh lime juice (about 3 large or 4 medium limes)

- 2 jalapeño peppers, seeded and minced

- 1 teaspoon chipotle chili powder, optional

- ½ cup chopped fresh cilantro

DIRECTIONS:

1. Prepare the boiling water canner. Heat the jars in simmering water until they're ready for use. Do not boil. Wash the lids in warm soapy water and set them aside with the bands.

2. Bring all the ingredients to a boil in a large stainless-steel or enameled saucepan. Reduce the heat and simmer for 5 to 10 minutes, stirring occasionally.

3. Ladle the hot salsa into a hot jar, leaving ½-inch of headspace. Remove the air bubbles. Wipe the jar rim clean. Center the lid on the jar. Apply the band and adjust to fingertip-tight. Place the jar in the boiling water canner. Repeat until all the jars are filled.

4. Process the jars for 15 minutes, adjusting for altitude. Turn off the heat; remove the lid, and let the jars stand for 5 minutes. Remove the jars and let them cool.

NUTRITION: Carbohydrates 76.29g; Fat 2.14g; Protein 6.13g; Calories 311

25. Bread and Butter Pickles

Preparation Time: 30 minutes

Cooking Time: 20 minutes

Servings: 3 quarts

INGREDIENTS:

- 15 cups of sliced pickling cucumbers, about 5 pounds; three cups for every pound
- 3 onions sliced thinly
- ¼ cup of salt
- 2 ½ cups of cider vinegar
- 2 ½ cups of sugar
- ¾ teaspoon of turmeric
- ½ teaspoon of celery seed
- 1 tablespoon of mustard seeds

- 6 cups of water

DIRECTIONS:

1. Mix the onions, ice, salt, and cucumbers together in a bowl.

2. Place a plate on top of the bowl with a gallon of water or something heavy on the plate. This serves as a weight. Let it stand for about three hours.

3. After three hours, rinse, and then drain.

4. Mix the sugar, vinegar, celery seed, mustard seed, and turmeric together in a large pot.

5. Add the drained cucumbers.

6. Bring the 6 cups of water almost to a boil in a pot on medium heat.

7. Right at boiling, remove from heat, and seal in the sterilized jars,

8. Place in a hot water bath for 10 minutes.

9. Dry them off, and place on a cookie sheet right side up for around 15 minutes in the oven at 225°F. This is done in order to ensure that there are no air pockets, that everything has been cooked right, and that it is sterilized and sealed properly before being stored. Let cool completely before storing.

NUTRITION: Carbohydrates 106.3g; Fat 5.76g; Protein 9.09g; Calories 492

Chapter 5: Pressure Canning: Fruits

26. Apple Sauce

Preparation Time: 30 minutes
Cooking Time: 20 minutes
Servings: 4 pints
INGREDIENTS:

- Mix for better flavor, different varieties together.
- 20 big apples
- 4 cups of water
- 2 1/2 cups of sugar

DIRECTIONS:

1. Wash apples; quarter, core; remove any blemishes or any other impurities.
2. If you work in larger lots, drop apples in lemon water, see on acidifying fruit.
3. Upon preparation of all apples, drain if necessary and place in a large cooking pot.
4. Add the four cups of water and cook until apples are soft over medium-high heat.
5. Press a colander to remove peels.
6. Return to the saucepan and add 2 1/2 cups of sugar.
7. Bring the mixture to a boil until the sugar dissolves completely.
8. Pack into boiling hot jars, leaving 1/2 inch of headspace.
9. Wipe the surface with the glass.
10. Screw the lids and rings with.
11. Run for 25 minutes in a boiling bath of water: both pints and quarts.

NUTRITION: Carbohydrates 188.03g; Fat 1.55g; Protein 2.37g; Calories 716

27. Pears

Preparation Time: 30 minutes

Cooking Time: 20 minutes

Servings: 7 half-pints

INGREDIENTS:

- 16 cups (16 medium-size pears) peeled & sliced fresh pears
- 3 tablespoons lemon juice
- 2 cups of water
- 4 cups of sugar

DIRECTIONS:

1. Combine the four ingredients in a large kettle and bring to a boil.
2. Uncover, cook, and stir often for 1 ½ to 2 hours until consistent.
3. Remove from stove and ladle the hot preserves into prepared seven hot sterilized jars with ¼-inch headspace.
4. Take out the air bubbles, make headspace adjustment, and wipe the rims while the center lids on the jars, and screw on the bands.
5. Place the jars in the boiling water in the canner and boil for ten minutes. Remove the hot jars; let cool on top of a towel.
6. Enjoy!

NUTRITION: Carbohydrates 21g; Fat 0g; Protein 0g

28. Strawberries

Preparation Time: 30 minutes

Cooking Time: 20 minutes

Servings: 7 half-pints

INGREDIENTS:

- 1 cup of sugar
- About 2 pounds of strawberries
- 1/2 cup of strawberry juice

DIRECTIONS:

1. Wash the strawberries.
2. Sort through berries, pick bruised, damaged, and too soft ones and put them aside.
3. Remove the roots, bruises, and damage from beers of poor quality.
4. Crush those berries and heat them up to get the juice.
5. Use a sieve to drain the juice from the berries.
6. Back to the pan.
7. Add sugar to the milk and simmer for 3 minutes.
8. Set aside to freshen up.
9. To canned stem berries; to put them in a large, non-reactive bowl or pot.
10. Set aside to about room temperature until juice has cooled.
11. Pour juice over berries, cover, and set aside for 3-5 hours, if the juice has cooled sufficiently.
12. Pack in jars to within 1/2 inch of the top after this point.

13. Make sure that juice is split evenly between the jars.

14. Screw and rings on the lid.

15. Add method in boiling bathwater: both 15 minutes of pints and quarts.

NUTRITION: Carbohydrates 26.52g; Fat 0.42g; Protein 0.92g; Calories 107

Chapter 6: Pressure Canning: Vegetables

29. Glazed Carrots

Preparation Time: 30 minutes

Cooking/pressurizing Time: 50 minutes

Servings: 6 pint jars (12 cups)

INGREDIENTS:

- 6-7 pounds of carrots

- 2 cups of brown sugar

- 2 cups of water

- 1 cup of orange juice

- 1 tablespoon kosher salt

DIRECTIONS:

1. Wash, peel, and slice carrots. Slices should be thick 1-2-inch. Mix brown sugar with water and orange juice as well as the carrots in a large saucepot. Bring to a boil. Reduce heat to medium, and

cook until the sugar has dissolved and carrots are almost tender about 10-15 minutes.

2. Pack the carrots into the jars, and pour the syrup over the carrots.

3. Process pints and quarts at 10 pounds each for 30 minutes for the weighted gauge of the pressure canner or 11 pounds if the pressure canner has a dial gauge.

4. Remove jars, and let them cool completely at room temperature before storing. This can take about a day.

NUTRITION: Carbohydrates 39.22g; Fat 0.47g; Protein 2.01g; Calories 161

30. Green Beans

Preparation Time: 30 minutes

Cooking Time: 20 minutes

Servings: 1 quart

INGREDIENTS:

- 2 lb. of green beans per quart
- Water
- Salt, optional
- Ball® Glass preserving jars with lids and bands

*You must process at least 2-quart jars or 4-pint jars in the pressure canner at one time to ensure safe processing.

DIRECTIONS:

1. Prepare pressure canner. Heat jars in simmering water until ready for use. Do not boil. Wash lids in warm soapy water and set bands aside.

2. Wash and rinse beans thoroughly. Remove string, trim ends and break or cut freshly gathered beans into 2-inch pieces. Place

prepared beans in a large saucepan and cover with boiling water. Boil for 5 minutes.

3. Pack hot beans into hot jars leaving 1-inch headspace. Add 1 tsp. salt to each quart jar, 1/2 tsp. to each pint jar, if desired.

4. Ladle boiling water over beans leaving 1-inch headspace. Remove air bubbles. Wipe rim. Center hot lid on jar. Apply band and adjust until fit is fingertip tight.

5. Process filled jars in a pressure canner at 10 pounds pressure 20 minutes for pints and 25 minutes for quarts, adjusting for altitude. Remove jars and cool. Check lids for seal after 24 hours. The lid should not flex up and down when the center is pressed.

TIP: The processing time given applies only to young, tender pods. Beans that have almost reached the "shell-out" stage require a longer time for processing. Increase processing time 15 minutes for pints and 20 minutes for quarts.

NUTRITION: Carbohydrates 33.16g; Fat 0.91g; Protein 6.35g; Calories 168

31. Tomatoes

Preparation Time: 30 minutes

Cooking Time: 20 minutes

Servings: 7 quarts

INGREDIENTS:

- 21 pounds whole tomatoes, skinned

- 4 tablespoons of salt

- ¾ cup lemon juice, optional

- Boiling water

DIRECTIONS:

1. Place the tomatoes and the salt in a saucepan and cover with the water. Bring to a boil and cook for 5 minutes.

2. Pack sterilized jars with the tomatoes and the hot liquid; leaving a ½ inch headspace, remove any air bubbles, clean the rim and adjust lids.

3. If omitting the lemon juice, process the jars for 45 minutes in a pressure canner at 10 pounds of pressure for a pressure canner with a weighted gauge or 11 pounds if the pressure canner has a dial gauge.

4. If using lemon juice, process the jars for 10 minutes in a boiling water bath.

NUTRITION: Carbohydrates 42.36g; Fat 3.6g; Protein 13.43g; Calories 210

32. Stewed Tomatoes

Preparation Time: 20 minutes

Cooking/pressurizing Time: 40 minutes

Servings: 4-pint jars or 2-quart jars

INGREDIENTS:

- 4 quarts red tomatoes, around 16-18 medium-size tomatoes
- 1 yellow onion, diced
- ½ green pepper, diced
- 4 teaspoons of celery salt
- 4 teaspoons of sugar
- 1 teaspoon of salt

DIRECTIONS:

1. Wash tomatoes. Blanch the tomatoes for 1-2 minutes in boiling water. Drain the water, and let cool until you can manipulate the

tomatoes with your fingers. Remove the skin, and chop the tomatoes.

2. Combine all ingredients into the saucepan, and bring to a boil. Reduce the heat to low. Cover, and let simmer gently for 12-15 minutes, stirring often, until it starts to get a bit thicker.

3. Pack the mixture equally into jars.

4. Process 15 minutes for pints at 11 pounds or 20 minutes for quarts at 10 pounds for the weighted gauge of the pressure canner or 11 pounds if the pressure canner has a dial gauge.

5. Remove the jars, and let cool until at room temperature before storing. This can take up to a day.

NUTRITION: Carbohydrates 9.59g; Fat 2.61g; Protein 1.42g; Calories 63

33. Herbed Peas

Preparation Time: 30 minutes

Cooking Time: 20 minutes

Servings: 4 pints

INGREDIENTS:

- 3 lbs. of peas
- Chervil
- Thyme
- Water

DIRECTIONS:

1. You will use the pressure canner with this one. Wash and dry peas and shell and wash again.
2. Boil the peas, pack hot peas in jars, and add seasoning and can using a pressure cooker.

NUTRITION: Carbohydrates 25.81g; Fat 0.69g; Protein 9.57g; Calories 143

34. Herbed Tomatoes

Preparation Time: 30 minutes

Cooking Time: 20 minutes

Servings: 4 pints

INGREDIENTS:

1. 8 lbs. tomatoes, peeled
2. Water
3. Spiced blend (house seasoning)

DIRECTIONS:

1. Combine tomatoes and water in a saucepan and let boil.
2. Add spices and add to canning tomatoes and use pressure cooking method.

NUTRITION: Carbohydrates 46.46g; Fat 4.2g; Protein 10.28g; Calories 238

35. Asparagus

Preparation Time: 30 minutes

Cooking Time: 20 minutes

Servings: 9 pints

INGREDIENTS:

- 16 pounds asparagus spears
- 10 tablespoons salt
- Boiling water

DIRECTIONS:

1. In a large pot, cover the asparagus with the boiling water and add the salt. Boil for 3 minutes. Fill sterilized jars loosely with the asparagus and liquid, leaving 1-inch headspace.

2. Adjust the jar lids and process the jars for 30 minutes in a pressure canner at 10 pounds of pressure for a pressure canner with a weighted gauge or 11 pounds if the pressure canner has a dial gauge.

NUTRITION: Carbohydrates 31.29g; Fat 0.97g; Protein 17.74g; Calories 161

36. Marinated Mushrooms

Preparation Time: 30 minutes

Cooking Time: 20 minutes

Servings: 9 pints

INGREDIENTS:

- Pimiento, diced (1/4 cup)

- Lemon juice, bottled (1/2 cup)

- Basil leaves, dried (1 tablespoon)

- White vinegar, 5% (2 ½ cups)

- Onions, chopped finely (1/2 cup)

- Mushrooms, small, whole (7 pounds)

- Oil, olive/salad (2 cups)

- Oregano leaves (1 tablespoon)

- Pickling/canning salt (1 tablespoon)

- Black peppercorns (25 pieces)

DIRECTIONS:

1. Make sure your mushrooms are very fresh, still unopened, and have caps with a diameter of less than 1 ¼ inches.

2. Wash the mushrooms before cutting the stems, but leave a quarter of an inch still attached to their caps. Put in a saucepan and cover with water and lemon juice. Heat until boiling, and then simmer for five minutes before draining.

3. Add the vinegar, salt, basil, oregano, and olive oil to a saucepan. Stir to combine as you also add the pimiento and onions. Heat the mixture until boiling.

4. Meanwhile, fill each of your clean and hot Mason jars (half-pint) with garlic clove (1/4 portion) and peppercorns (2 to 3 pieces)/ Add the cooked mushrooms as well as the hot liquid mixture, making sure to leave half an inch of headspace.

5. Take out any air bubbles before adjusting the lids. Place in the pressure canner and process for twenty minutes.

TIPS: You can process your foods without salt. Use canning salt if you want to add salt to your pressure canned foods. You can add one-half teaspoon of canning salt to each pint jar (if using quart jars, add one teaspoon).

NUTRITION: Carbohydrates 2.97g; Fat 48.25g; Protein 0.49g; Calories 451

Chapter 7: Pressure Canning: Meat, Poultry, and Seafood

37. Canned Chicken

Preparation Time: 30 minutes

Cooking/pressurizing Time: 2 hours

Servings: 8-pint jars

INGREDIENTS:

- 18 medium boneless and skinless chicken breasts
- 1 ½ tablespoon of salt
- 4 ½ cups of water
- Butter or Olive Oil for frying in a skillet

DIRECTIONS:

1. Cook each side of the chicken in a skillet with some butter or olive oil, about 8-10 minutes. Remove from heat when the chicken is white and cooked all the way through. If you poke it with a fork, the juices run clear.

2. In each pint jar place a ½ teaspoon of salt and 2 chicken breasts.

3. Fill the jar with water, process for 70 minutes at 10 pounds of pressure for the weighted gauge of the pressure canner or 11 pounds if the pressure canner has a dial gauge.

4. Remove jars, and let cool until it is room temperature, which may take about a day.

NUTRITION: Carbohydrates 0g; Fat 55.09g; Protein 5.06g; Calories 509

38. Mexican Turkey Soup

Preparation Time: 20 minutes

Cooking/pressurizing Time: 1 hour and 30 minutes

Servings: 8-quart jars or 16-pint jars

INGREDIENTS:

- 6 cups of cooked turkey, chopped
- 2 cups of chopped onions
- 8 ounces can of Mexican green chilies, chopped and drained
- ¼ cup of taco seasoning mix, packed
- 28 ounces of crushed tomatoes with the juices
- 16 cups of turkey or chicken broth
- 3 cups of corn
- 1 ½ tablespoon of extra virgin olive oil

DIRECTIONS:

1. In a large stockpot, warm olive oil on medium-high heat. Sauté the onions until tender and fragrant, about 2 minutes on medium-high heat. Reduce heat to medium-low.

2. Add taco seasoning and the chilies. Cook and stir for another 3 minutes, add in the tomatoes and the broth. Bring to a boil, and then add the corn and the turkey.

3. Reduce heat to low, and let simmer for 10 minutes.

4. Ladle equally into the jars.

5. Process pints at 10 pounds for 75 minutes and quarts at 10 pounds for 90 minutes for the weighted gauge of the pressure canner or 11 pounds if the pressure canner has a dial gauge.

6. Remove jars, and let cool until it is at room temperature. This may take about a day.

NUTRITION: Carbohydrates 30.08g; Fat 76.84g; Protein 63.66g; Calories 1079

39. Fish

Preparation Time: 20 minutes

Cooking/pressurizing Time: 1 hour and 30 minutes

Servings: 5 pints

INGREDIENTS:

- 5 pounds tuna or salmon
- 5-pint sized mason jars with lids and rings
- Canning salt
- Lemon juice
- 1 jalapeño pepper

DIRECTIONS:

1. Place 1 slice of jalapeño pepper into each jar.
2. Fill jars with meat to ½ inch from the top.
3. Add ¼ tsp. canning salt and 1 tsp. lemon juice per pint.
4. Use a knife to jiggle meat and remove any air pockets.
5. Wipe rim of jar clean.
6. Heat lids in hot water for 3 minutes; place lids on jars and tighten rings slightly.
7. Place jars in the canner and fill with water to the jar rings.
8. Close and lock pressure canner and bring to a boil over high heat, then add cooking weight to the top.
9. After 20 minutes, turn heat to medium and cook for 75 minutes.
10. Turn off heat and leave canner alone until it has cooled completely to room temperature.

11. After canner has cooled, remove jars from the canner and check for sealing.

12. If jars have sealed, store for up to 2 years; if not, use meat right away.

NUTRITION: Carbohydrates 1.51g; Fat 32.56g; Protein 93.79g; Calories 700

40. Chicken Cacciatore

Preparation time: 20 minutes

Cooking time: 20 minutes

Servings: 8-10 pints

INGREDIENTS:

- 3 tablespoons olive oil
- 8 large breasts boneless, skinless chicken breasts, cut into 2-inch cubes (8 cups)
- 12 boneless, skinless chicken thighs, cut into 2-inch pieces (6 cups)
- 1 tablespoon dried oregano
- 1 tablespoon dried basil
- 1 teaspoon dried thyme
- 1 teaspoon dried rosemary, crushed
- 1 teaspoon coarse sea salt
- ½ teaspoon ground black pepper
- 1 cup red wine
- 4 cups diced tomatoes, with their juice
- 4 cups tomato juice
- 2 cups sliced white mushrooms
- 3 cups coarsely chopped sweet onion
- 1 large red bell pepper, chopped (1½ cups)
- 1 celery stalk, chopped (½ cup)
- 6 garlic cloves, minced
- ¾ cup tomato paste (6 ounces)
- 1 tablespoon granulated sugar

DIRECTIONS:

1. In a thick-bottomed stockpot, combine the oil and the chicken breasts and thighs. Mix well to coat the chicken. Cook the chicken on medium-high heat for 3 minutes, stirring often. Add

the oregano, basil, thyme, rosemary, salt, and pepper. Mix well and cook for an additional 3 minutes. Add the red wine, cover the stockpot, and let cook for 5 more minutes undisturbed.

2. Add the tomatoes, Tomato Juice, mushrooms, onion, bell pepper, celery, and garlic. Mix well and bring to a boil. Boil for 5 minutes. Add the tomato paste and sugar, mixing well to distribute paste. Boil for an additional 5 minutes. Remove from the heat.

3. Using a slotted spoon, fill each hot jar three-quarters full with the chicken and vegetables. Ladle the hot tomato sauce over the mixture, leaving 1 inch of headspace. Remove any air bubbles and add additional sauce if necessary to maintain the 1 inch of headspace.

4. Wipe the rim of each jar with a warm washcloth dipped in distilled white vinegar. Place a lid and ring on each jar and hand tighten.

5. Place jars in the pressure canner, lock the pressure canner lid and bring to a boil on high heat. Let the canner vent for 10 minutes. Close the vent and continue heating to achieve 11 PSI for a dial gauge and 10 PSI for a weighted gauge. Process quart jars for 1 hour 30 minutes and pint jars for 1 hour 15 minutes.

Serving Tip: This dish is traditionally served over pasta noodles, flat or spaghetti, and topped with fresh chopped parsley and shaved Parmesan cheese. For a fun kick, use V8® juice, regular or spicy, instead of Tomato Juice.

NUTRITION: Carbohydrates 42.14g; Fat 43.8g; Protein 37.12g; Calories 701

Chapter 8: Pressure Canning: Soups, Stews

41. Cabbage Soup

Preparation time: 30 minutes
Cooking time: 1 hour and 15 minutes
Servings: 9 pints

INGREDIENTS:

- 2 kg of minced meat
- 1 large onion, diced
- 2 garlic cloves, minced
- 6 cups of cabbage, grated
- 1 cup diced celery
- 1 cup diced green pepper
- 2 cans of light beans (16 ounces)
- 8 glasses of canned tomatoes with juice (2 liters if you can make your own like me)
- 10 cubes of veal broth
- 8 cups of water
- 2 tablespoons of garlic powder
- 20 rounds of fresh peppercorn (I use it)
- 2 teaspoons of sea salt
- 1 tablespoon of dried parsley
- 2 tablespoons of dried basil
- 1 tablespoon of thyme
- 1 teaspoon dried celery

DIRECTIONS:

Sterilizing

- Sterilize to prepare glass jars, lids, and rings. Chop and cut all the vegetables and set aside. Collect all the dry ingredients and set them aside

Cooking:

1. **Minced meat:** brown minced meat in a pan so far pink. Separate 3 tablespoons of onion and garlic fat. If desired, drain and wash the meat to remove excess oil.

2. **Prepare the beef:** heat 8 cups of water in a large bowl or use 2-liter jars filled with water in each jar - 5 cubes of beef broth.

3. Microwave for 5 minutes to dissolve the cubes. Remove it carefully, it will be very hot, stir quickly to make sure the cubes are thawed.

4. **Sautéed onion and garlic:** pour 3 tablespoons of fat in a large saucepan and wrap the chopped onions and fry the garlic until tender.

5. **Mix with other ingredients:** add cooked minced meat, cabbage, celery, green pepper, beans, fruit juice, tomato, and broth - mix well.

6. **Mix all the dry ingredients:** garlic powder, pepper, sea salt, parsley, basil, thyme, and celery. Boil, and cook for 20 minutes. Actually, your soup is ready to eat at this point.

Filling jars:

- **Note:** protect the counter by using a cloth or towel to adjust the jars since you will fill the hot jars. Make use of a spoon strainer to fill the jars with half-filled solids, then fill the rest of the jar with water up to 1 inch in the cavity. Using a clean, damp cloth, remove any particles or water from the edge of the glass jar, insert the lid and ring and squeeze with your finger. When filling each can, place it in the pressure container. Make sure to place the shelf under the can.

Processing:

7. Place the lid on the box and lock it. Set the temperature to high. Vent the steam for it

NUTRITION: Carbohydrates 101.88g; Fat 7.44g; Protein 88.47g; Calories 773

42. Beef Stew

Preparation time: 30 minutes
Cooking time: 15 minutes
Servings: 7 quarts or 14 pints
INGREDIENTS:

- 2 tablespoons of extra-virgin olive oil, divided
- 5 pounds of stew beef, cut into bite-size pieces
- 10 cups of potatoes, peeled and cubed
- 8 cups of medium carrots, peeled and chopped
- 3 cups of chopped onions
- 2 cups of chopped celery
- 6 medium Roma tomatoes, diced (3 cups)
- 4½ teaspoons of coarse sea salt (optional)
- 1 tablespoon of dried parsley
- 1 tablespoon of dried oregano
- ½ tablespoon of celery seeds
- 1 teaspoon of ground coriander
- 1 teaspoon of dried thyme
- 1 teaspoon of dried basil
- ½ teaspoon of ground black pepper
- 8 cups of Beef Broth
- 5 cups of water

DIRECTIONS:

1. In a thick-bottomed stockpot, heat 1 tablespoon oil and brown the beef in batches until all the beef is lightly browned, about 3 to 5 minutes per batch. Add 1 additional tablespoon of oil while browning each batch. Remove each batch from the stockpot and place it in a bowl. Be sure not to fully cook the beef.

2. Return the browned beef to the stockpot and add the potatoes, carrots, onions, celery, tomatoes, salt (if using), parsley, oregano, celery seeds, coriander, thyme, basil, and pepper and mix well. Add the Beef Broth and water and mix well. Bring to a boil over medium-high heat, stirring frequently. Let it boil for 5 minutes then remove from the heat.

3. Ladle the hot stew into hot jars, leaving 1 inch of headspace. Remove any air bubbles and add additional stew if necessary, to maintain the 1 inch of headspace.

4. Wipe the rim of each jar with a warm washcloth dipped in distilled white vinegar. Place a lid and ring on each jar and hand tighten.

5. Place jars in the pressure canner, lock the pressure canner lid and bring to a boil on high heat. Let the canner vent for 10 minutes. Close the vent and continue heating to achieve 11 PSI for a dial gauge and 10 PSI for a weighted gauge. Process quart jars for 1 hour 30 minutes and pint jars for 1 hour 15 minutes.

INGREDIENT TIP: Using a pressure canner makes even the toughest cuts of meat tender and flavorful. Beef sold for stew typically comes from the chuck or round roasts, cut into 1½-inch pieces. Bottom and eye cuts, also known as round, are typically leaner than a chuck roast, which are cuts from the shoulder, leg, and butt. When cutting into bite-size pieces, cut to a size you would feel comfortable seeing on the end of your fork or spoon.

NUTRITION: Carbohydrates 55.14g; Fat 16.38g; Protein 81.16g; Calories 680

43. Potato and Leek Soup

Preparation time: 30 minutes

Cooking time: 15 minutes

Servings: 7 quarts or 14 pints

INGREDIENTS:

- 6 potatoes, peeled and cubed

- 4 cups stock, chicken or beef

- 5 pounds leeks, washed and cut into ¼-inch slices

DIRECTIONS:

1. Layer leaks at the bottom of each jar. Place a layer of potatoes on top of the leeks, followed by another layer of the sliced leeks.

2. Boil the chicken or beef stock before pouring into the jars. Make sure to leave about an inch of space at the top of each jar.

3. Attach the lids to the jars and process in a pressure canner using 11 pounds for 60 minutes.

NUTRITION: Carbohydrates 101.1g; Fat 2.34g; Protein 14.26g; Calories 462

44. Veggie Soup

Preparation time: 60 minutes

Cooking time: 15 minutes

Servings: 9-pint jars

INGREDIENTS:

- 6 cups tomatoes (cored, peeled, chopped)
- 2 cups of tomatillos (chopped)
- 1 cup of onion (chopped)
- 1 cup of carrots (chopped)
- 1 cup of green bell pepper (chopped)
- 1 cup of red bell pepper (chopped)
- 6 cups of corn kernels
- ½ cup hot pepper (seeded, chopped)
- 1 teaspoon cayenne pepper
- 5 cups tomato juice
- 1 tablespoon hot sauce
- 2 teaspoon chili powder
- 2 teaspoon cumin (ground)
- 1 teaspoon salt
- 2 cups of water
- 1 teaspoon black pepper

DIRECTIONS:

1. Sterilize the jars
2. Combine all the ingredients in a pot and bring to boil.
3. Simmer uncovered for 15 minutes on low flame.
4. Distribute the solids and liquid among the jars, leaving one inch of headspace.
5. Get rid of any air bubbles and clean the rims.

6. Cover the jars with the lid and apply the bands making sure that it is tightened.

7. Process the jars for 60 minutes at 10 pounds pressure in a pressure canner.

8. Remove; allow cooling, and then labeling the jars.

NUTRITION: Calories: 185; Fat: 1.9g; Carbohydrates: 42.8g; Proteins: 6.9g

45. Fennel & Carrot Soup

Preparation time: 35 minutes

Cooking time: 30 minutes

Servings: 9-pint jars

INGREDIENTS:

- 1 lb. of fennel bulbs (trimmed)
- 1 tablespoon of olive oil
- 4 ½ lbs. of carrots (peeled, sliced)
- 12 cups of vegetable stock
- 2 teaspoon of onion powder
- 2 tablespoons of salt
- 1 teaspoon of dried ginger (ground)
- 1 teaspoon of dried thyme
- ½ teaspoon of cumin (ground)
- 3 tablespoons of lemon juice
- 1 teaspoon of black pepper (ground)
- 1 teaspoon of dried coriander (ground)

DIRECTIONS:

1. Sterilize the jars
2. Heat oil in a pot and sauté the fennel in it till translucent.
3. Mix in the carrots and 4 cups vegetable broth and simmer for 30 minutes.
4. Leave to cool, and then puree the mixture.
5. Return to the pot and mix in the remainder of the ingredients.
6. Bring to boil and simmer for 20-30 minutes.

7. Ladle the mix immediately into the sterilized jars, leaving one inch of headspace.

8. Get rid of any air bubbles and clean the rims.

9. Cover the jars with the lid and apply the bands making sure that it is tightened.

10. Process the jars for 35 minutes at 10 pounds pressure in a pressure canner.

11. Remove; allow cooling, and then labeling the jars.

NUTRITION: Calories 48; Fat 0.7g; Carbohydrates 10.1g; Proteins 2.8g

46. Tomato Soup

Preparation time: 30 minutes

Cooking time: 20 minutes

Servings: 18-pint jars

INGREDIENTS:

- 15 lbs. of tomatoes (chopped roughly)
- 2 tablespoons of olive oil
- 3 cups of celery (chopped)
- 3 cups of onions (chopped)
- 1 tablespoon of salt
- 1 tablespoon of pepper
- 64 oz. of vegetable stock
- ¼ cup of garlic (chopped)
- 32 oz. of water
- 2 cups of carrots (chopped)

DIRECTIONS:

1. Sterilize the jars
2. Heat olive oil in a pot and sauté the onions, celery, and carrots in it.
3. Mix in the tomatoes, salt, pepper, stock, and water and leave to simmer for 2 hours.
4. Pour the soup using an immersion blender.
5. Ladle the mix immediately into the sterilized jars, leaving one inch of headspace.
6. Get rid of any air bubbles and clean the rims.

7. Cover the jars with the lid and apply the bands making sure that it is tightened.

8. Submerge the jars within a prepared boiling water canner and leave to process for 20 minutes.

9. Remove; allow cooling, and then labeling the jars.

NUTRITION: Calories: 63.4; Fat: 1.7g; Carbohydrates: 10g; Proteins: 1.8g

47. Chicken Soup

Preparation time: 30 minutes
Cooking time: 20 minutes
Servings: 8-pint jars
INGREDIENTS:

- 3 cups of chicken (diced)
- 6 cups of chicken broth
- 10 cups of water
- 1 cup of onion (diced)
- Salt and pepper to taste
- 1 ½ cups of celery (diced)
- 1 ½ cups of carrots (sliced)
- 3 chicken bouillon cubes

DIRECTIONS:

1. Sterilize the jars
2. Combine all the ingredients in a pot except the salt, pepper, and bouillon cubes and bring to boil.
3. Reduce the flame and simmer for 30 minutes.
4. Stir in the remaining ingredients and stir cook until the bouillon cubes dissolve.
5. Turn off the flame and skim-off any visible foam.
6. Ladle the mix immediately into the sterilized jars, leaving one inch of headspace.
7. Get rid of any air bubbles and clean the rims.
8. Cover the jars with the lid and apply the bands making sure that it is tightened.
9. Process the jars for 1 hour 15 minutes at 10 pounds pressure in a pressure canner.
10. Remove; allow cooling, and then labeling the jars.

NUTRITION: Calories: 75.4; Fat: 0.3g; Carbohydrates: 5.4g; Proteins: 12.2g

Chapter 9: Fermenting

The Process of Fermentation

Food Fermentation isn't rocket science. You don't need to have a food fermentation factory to do so, and you also don't need lots of cash just to be able to ferment food. In fact, you can do it in the comforts of your own home and that's one of the best things about it.

So, how exactly can you ferment food? What are the basic ways of doing so? Here's what you need to know:

1. **Choose your equipment.** Of course, before you start the process of food fermentation, you should first have the right equipment with you. Mason Jars are definitely needed, as well as good kinds of knives that you can use to prepare the vegetables. Most of the equipment that you may need are as follows:

- **Fermenting Vessel.** This is where you'll place those vegetables or condiments. It's a general rule that cylindrical-shaped containers are better than other shapes because it's easier to ferment in them. Examples of Fermenting Vessels include:

    1. Ceramic Crocks
    2. Ceramic Fermenting Crocks
    3. Canning Jars
    4. Slow Cooker Inserts
    5. Mason/Glass Jars
    6. Ceramic or Glass Bowls
    7. Glass Jars with Airlock Systems

- **Weights and Covers**. You also need equipment that will cover the food for you and this always depends on what food you'll be fermenting. For example, Vegetables in brine are required to have weight and cover systems, whereas vegetables, fruits, and condiments without brine can be prepared simply by just placing a lid on the container and waiting for them to be fermented. Examples of Weights and Covers include:
    1. Ceramic Fermentation Weights
    2. Heavy Glass
    3. Ceramic Coasters
    4. Small jars
    5. Small plates

2. **Method of Preparation**. Next, you should also decide on which method of preparation you'll use to ferment the food that you have on hand. This differs based on the ingredients that you have with you and you have to know which method is best suited for what you have with you. Some of these methods are:

- **Chopping.** When you chop vegetables or fruits, you have to be sure that they'll be in bite-sized pieces, so you can easily eat them right away. Examples of vegetables that you can chop include summer squash, cucumber, peppers, green beans, asparagus, eggplant, and carrots.

- **Grating.** Grated fruits or vegetables are very smooth and come only in extremely small but somewhat lengthy pieces. You can either do this by hand or with the help of a food processor. Usually, these are done for those that you want to make as relish or sides. Examples include cabbage, zucchini, cucumber, beets, turnips, radish, and carrot.

- **Slicing.** Slicing fruits or vegetables increases surface area and is best done for Sauerkraut and those fruits or vegetables that you'll soak in the brine. They also make culturing time faster. Examples include celery, peppers, zucchini, cucumbers, and cabbage.

3. **Culturing**. Culturing, or the use of whey, salt, and other kinds of starters is the act of choosing which starter culture is best for whatever it is that you want to make. Oftentimes, they determine the length of time for those foods to be fermented and you need starter cultures to inhibit the growth of undesirable bacteria or organisms that may stall the fermentation process. Examples of starter cultures include:

- **Salt**. Salt has always been the classic culture for fermenting food and it has been used even before refrigeration was around. Salt pulls undesired bacteria away and takes moisture out of the food that you're preparing so that it will last for a long time. It also suppresses the growth of organisms that you don't actually need. 1 to 3 Tablespoons of salt for every quart of water is the recommended ratio.

- **Fermented Juice**. Basically, this is the juice or the liquid taken from food that you have fermented earlier. You just have to add around ¼ cup of it to the new mixture, together with salt brine to make fermentation easier.

- **Whey**. Whey is kind of tricky because it may work for others but may not work for the rest. If you're going to use whey, make sure that it tastes fresh and that it has been strained properly. Whey's great though, in the sense that it keeps the natural crunchiness of vegetables intact.

4. **Water Source**. It's a given fact that you need brine to ferment most types of food, but where exactly should the water you'll use come from? Here are some water sources that you can choose from:

- **Tap Water**. Basically, tap water is water that comes out of the faucet. It can either be mineral-rich or on the other hand, it could also be free of any minerals. You may have to run this through a water softener first just to make sure that it's safe.

- **Spring Water**. Spring water usually comes in bottles but is originally from the ground—which makes it rich in minerals and makes it healthy!

- **Distilled Water**. Distilled Water contains no minerals and has been thoroughly purified. You can usually buy this from your water supply store or from the supermarket.

- **Bottled Water.** This can either be mineral water, spring or distilled. Just check the label to be sure what of it is.

5. **Keeping them safe**. When you're trying to ferment vegetables, you want to be sure that they stay in place so that the fermentation process won't be interrupted. Some of the things that you can use to keep them safe are:

- **A small dish**. Put a small dish on top of the vegetables and make sure that brine covers it as well. Then, place another small heavy item on top of the dish to keep it even safer.

- **Cabbage or Kale leaf.** Actually, any strong piece of a vegetable leaf will do. Just tuck it on top of the vegetables and it will already be able to keep the vegetables in place. Carrot or Zucchini strips can work, too.

- **Ceramic Fermentation Weights.** These are basically made for the process of fermentation so you can never go wrong with them.

- **Glass Stones.** You know, those stones that you usually use to decorate the aquarium or your floral arrangements with—they are these stones. Make sure though that they're really clean before you put them on top of the vegetables. Choose ones that are over 2 inches in diameter, so you won't have a hard time.

- **Fermenting in a bowl before transferring to jars.** If you can't make use of the methods given above, it's also okay to ferment the vegetables in a bowl first then just use a large plate to press them down. Once they're done or are fully submerged, move them to the storage jars together with their brine.

6. **Ready for the move.** Finally, once you have done all the techniques above, it's time for the vegetables to be transferred into cold storage. However, this may be tricky because not everyone knows if the food's actually ready to be moved or not. Well, here are some signs that will allow you to know if you can already transfer the vegetables to cold storage:

- **The Smell.** It's true that you'll know whether a food is good or not through its aroma. Well, you'll also know whether a food is already close to being fermented or not by means of smelling it and by the aroma that it emits. If your fermented food is ready, it should have this vinegary-sour smell. At first, the smell may be too strong, then you'll notice that it will subside after a couple of seconds or so. However, when you think that it smells rotten, chances are it probably is, so just throw it away and start all over again.

- **Bubbles.** Seeing bubbles in your fermented foods are also normal because it means that lactic acid has been formed and that the vegetables are being cultured. Take note though, that the amount and size of bubbles will differ for each food product so know that even though zucchini has more bubbles than tomatoes, there's no problem with it.

- **Flavor.** And of course, the flavor is very important, too. Now, when you've smelled that sour smell and when you've seen the bubbles, you should get on to taste what you have made. Once you notice that it's already flavorful or tangy, especially for pickles, you can then transfer them to cold storage. Congratulations!

7. **And, beware of molds.** As you're going to ferment these fruits and vegetables, you should also be aware that molds may form, and once they do, you have to discard what you have made and just begin again. Molds usually appear because of a variety of things and some of them are:

- **The Quality of Fruits and Vegetables.** Of course, when you see that the fruits and vegetables you have on hand are about to decay, why in the world would you still use them? That's just like you're inviting molds to invade them!

- **The amount of salt**. 1 to 3 Tablespoons of salt per quart of water is good, but anything more (or less) than that may just bring on bad bacteria and molds, so always be aware of how much salt you're putting in.

- **Vegetable Submersion**. You can prevent molds from infesting your vegetables if you actually submerge them well in water and if you won't allow oxygen to come in contact with them while they're in the fermenting vessel.

- **The Temperature**. It's best to ferment food in a cool place because this will prevent molds from being around, and it'll also make the whole process faster and easier. 65 to 70F is recommended.

Fermenting

Chapter 10: Freezing

Freezing and refrigeration are the most common types of preservation in homes around the world today. Where refrigeration slows bacterial action, freezing comes close to totally stopping microbes' development. This happens because the water in frozen food turns to ice, in which bacteria cannot continue to grow. Enzyme activity, on the other hand, isn't completely deterred by freezing, which is why many vegetables are blanched before being packaged. Once an item is defrosted completely, however, any microbes still within will begin to grow again.

What Can Be Frozen?

Except for eggs in the shell, nearly all foods can be frozen raw, after blanching and/or cooking. So the real question here is what foods don't take well to freezing. The following list includes the foods you generally cannot freeze:

- Cream sauces separate even when warmed completely after being frozen.

- Mayonnaise, cream cheese, and cottage cheese don't hold up well, often losing textural quality.

- Milk seems to be a 50-50 proposition. While it can be frozen quite safely, it sometimes separates after being frozen. If remixed, this milk is an option for cooking and baking.

- Precooked meat can be frozen, but it doesn't have as much moisture as raw and will often dry out further if left frozen for more than four weeks.

- Cured meats don't last long in the freezer and should be used in less than four weeks.

If you're ever in doubt about how to best prepare an item for freezing (or even if you should), the National Center for Home Preserving **(www.uga.edu/nchfp)** is a great online resource. It offers tips on how to freeze various items ranging from pie and prepared food to oysters and artichokes.

Frosty Facts

In freezing, zero is your magic number. At 0°F, microbes become dormant. The food won't spoil, and any germs therein will not breed until you defrost the food. Bear in mind, though, that the longer the food remains frozen the more it tends to lose certain qualities such as vivid flavor and texture. Always try to freeze things when they're at their peak and remember that cooking your defrosted food as soon as it's thawed will also stop microbial growth.

The first step in freezing is keeping those items cold until you're ready to prepare them. This is very important with meat, but it also makes a difference in how fruits and vegetables come out of the freezer.

1. Equipment

Once you're ready to begin, assemble all the items you need. For example, if you're freezing fruit, you'll want a clean cutting board, a sharp knife, and your choice of storage containers. If you're doing any preparation on the fruit before freezing it, you'll also need cooking pans. Stainless steel is highly recommended; galvanized pans may give off zinc when the fruit is left in them because of the fruit's acid content. Additionally, there's nothing like stainless steel for easy cleanup.

If it's in your budget, a vacuum sealer is another great piece of equipment to consider. Vacuum sealers come in a variety of sizes with a similar variety of bags that are perfect for preservers who like freezing and drying methods. They're fairly cost-effective when compared to freezer bags or plastic containers, and they eliminate the excess air that contributes to ice crystals.

A third item that you shouldn't be without is a freezer-proof label system. If you double-wrap your frozen items, put a label on each layer. If one gets knocked off, the other remains.

2. Help and Hints

Freezing, like any other method of preservation, requires some observation and annotation to achieve success. As you're working with recipes, remember that practice really does make perfect. For example, you may follow a recipe for frozen butter pickles exactly, but you find you'd like the cucumbers sliced more thinly for greater flavor. Make a note of that and change it next time.

As you note changes you'd like to make, also consider if that means getting different types of equipment for your kitchen. In the case of the cucumbers and other thinly sliced vegetables, a mandolin might be the perfect fix. Put it on a wish list. Being prepared saves a lot of last-minute headaches, and having the right tools is always a great boon.

3. Vegetables

Vegetables should be chosen for crispness and freshness. Home gardeners should pick their items a few hours before packing them for the ultimate in organic goodness. The next step for vegetables is blanching, which will improve the lifespan of your frozen goods.

If there's no specific blanching time provided in your preserving recipe, here's a brief overview to get you started. Remember to move your vegetables into an ice bath immediately after blanching until they're totally cooled.

Timing and Techniques for Blanching Vegetables

- **Asparagus.** Remove the tough ends from the asparagus. Depending on the storage container, you may need to cut the stems in half. If your stalks are thin, they'll only need 2 minutes of blanching; thick stalks require twice as much.

- **Beans (green or wax).** Remove any tips. Leave the beans whole and blanch them for 3 minutes.

- **Brussels sprouts.** Clean off outer leaves, then soak the sprouts in cold salty water for 30 minutes. Drain and blanch for 4 minutes.

- **Cabbage.** Remove the outer leaves. Shred the cabbage and blanch for just over 1 minute and leave in the water for another 30 seconds before icing.

- **Carrots.** Clean the skins, then slice into ¼ pieces. Blanch for 3 minutes. Whole baby carrots need 5 minutes of blanching.

- **Cauliflower and broccoli.** Break off the pieces from the central core and clean well (a spray nozzle at the sink works very well). Soak in a gallon of salty water (3–4 teaspoons salt) for 30 minutes. Pour off the liquid. Rinse and blanch for 3 minutes.

- **Corn.** Rinse, remove from the cob, and blanch for 5 minutes.

- **Mushrooms (small).** These can be frozen whole. Toss with a little fresh lemon juice and blanch for 4 minutes.

- **Greens (including spinach).** Rinse. Remove any leaves that have spots or other damage. Blanch for 3 minutes.

- **Peas.** Blanch out of the husk for 90 seconds.

- **Peas in the pod.** Trim the ends and remove strings. Blanch for 1–2 minutes, depending on the size of the pod.

- **Peppers.** Slice open and remove the seeds. Cut into the desired size and blanch for 2 minutes.

- **Potatoes.** Wash and scrub thoroughly. Remove the peel and blanch for 4 minutes.

- **Tomatoes.** To easily peel the skins, use a straining spoon and dip the tomatoes in boiling water for 30 seconds. Peel and remove the core. These can be stored whole or diced to desired size.

- **Zucchini and squash.** Peel. Cut into ½-inch slices and blanch for 3 minutes.

Fruit

Do small batches of fruit so it doesn't brown while you're packing. Fruit need not be packed in syrup, but many people do prefer the texture and taste that sugar or sugar syrup adds to frozen fruit. Some folks use sugar substitutes for dietary reasons. In any case, small fruits such as berries take well to a simple sprinkling. Larger chunks such as peaches do well in syrup. The average ratio is ½ cup of syrup to every pint of fruit. Some preservers like to use ascorbic acid to improve the quality of frozen fruit.

Adding about ½ teaspoon of this per pint is sufficient; just mix it into the syrup or a little water.

Packaging

Since 95 percent of American homes freeze some of their food regularly, it's not surprising to find people have a lot of questions on the best type of storage containers to use and how to prepare food for the table after it's been frozen. Plastic bags are the most common receptacles, followed by plastic containers. While some people have been known to use glass, this is a bit risky since the glass may crack and break when the food inside expands in the freezing process. Additionally, slippery glass jars coming out of the freezer are easily dropped.

Overall, it's always a good idea to use bags and containers that are rated for freezing. Avoid using waxed cartons; they don't retain the food's quality very well and defrosted food often becomes limp and unstable for handling. Your packaging materials should also be leak and oil resistant, and all packing materials should be able to withstand freezing.

1. **Size Counts**

Another consideration with your containers is size. Think about how many people you plan to serve and choose freezing containers accordingly. If you're going to put several servings in one large container, separate them with a piece of aluminum foil or plastic wrap so you can take out one at a time fairly easily.

2. **Space Constraints**

When you're packing food into a container, always leave a little room for expansion. Let the food reach room temperature before you freeze it (right out of the ice bath is a perfect time with vegetables). Putting warm or hot food in the freezer creates a temperature variance for all the food inside the freezer.

Most importantly, remember to label and date everything. This will help you gauge what should be eaten first so it retains the greatest quality.

3. Wrap It Up

Many preservers wrap the meat with aluminum foil or freezer wrap, then transfer it into another freezer bag or container. This decreases the chance that water crystals will form and protects the foil from being accidentally torn. Note, however, that waxed paper isn't a good choice for freezing because it doesn't resist moisture.

4. Stews and Leftovers

If you know in advance that you'd like to set aside some of what you're cooking for the freezer, it's a good idea to leave it a little undercooked. Freeze the goods as soon as they reach room temperature. When you warm it up, you will finish the cooking process and can also doctor the flavor a bit at that time. Your frozen foods need not be defrosted before you start cooking them. Just remember to get all the packing materials off the item first—you would not be the first person to forget this step and find unpleasant paper or wrapping in a meat serving!

Freezing

Chapter 11: Canning and Preserving Safety Tips

There are a few safety tips that you should follow when you start canning and preserving foods from home. Canning is a great way to store and preserve foods, but it can be risky if not done correctly. However, if you follow these tips, you will be able to can foods in a safe manner.

- **Choose the Right Canner**

The first step to safe home canning is choosing the right canner. First off, know when to use a pressure canner or a water bath canner.

Use a pressure canner that is specifically designed for canning and preserving foods. There are several types of canner out there and some are just for cooking food, not for preserving food and processing jars. Be sure that you have the right type of equipment.

Make sure your pressure canner is the right size. If your canner is too small, the jars may be undercooked. Always opt for a larger canner as the pressure on the bigger pots tends to be more accurate, and you will be able to take advantage of the larger size and can more foods at once!

Before you begin canning, check that your pressure canner is in good condition. If your canner has a rubber gasket, it should be flexible and soft. If the rubber is dry or cracked, it should be replaced before you start canning. Be sure your canner is clean and the small vents in the lid are free of debris. Adjust your canner for high altitude processing if needed.

Once you are sure your canner is ready to go and meets all these guidelines, it is time to start canning!

- **Opt for a Screw Top Lid System**

There are many kinds of canning jars that you can choose to purchase. However, the only type of jar that is approved by the USDA is a mason jar with a screw-top lid. These are designated "preserving jars" and are considered the safest and most effective option for home preserving uses.

Some jars are not thought to be safe for home preservation despite being marketed as canning jars. Bail Jars, for example, have a two-part wire clasp lid with a rubber ring in between the lid and jar. While these were popular in the past, it is now thought that the thick rubber and tightly closed lid does not provide a sufficient seal, leading to a higher potential for botulism. Lightening Jars should not be used for canning as they are simply glass jars with glass lids, with no rubber at all. That will not create a good seal!

Reusing jars from store-bought products is another poor idea. They may look like they're in good condition, but they are typically designed to be processed in a commercial facility. Most store-bought products do not have the two-part band and lid system which is best for home canning. Also, the rubber seal on a store-bought product is likely not reusable once you open the original jar. You can reuse store-bought jars at home for storage but not for canning and preserving.

- **Check Your Jars, Lids, and Bands**

As you wash your jars with soapy water, check for any imperfections. Even new jars may have a small chip or crack and need to be discarded. You can reuse jars again and again as long as they are in good condition.

The metal jar rings are also reusable; however, you should only reuse them if they are rust free and undented. If your bands begin to show signs of wear, consider investing in some new ones.

Jar lids need to be new as the sealing compound on the lid can disintegrate over time. When you store your jars in damp places (like in a basement or canning cellar) the lids are even more likely to disintegrate. Always use new lids to ensure that your canning is successful.

- **Check for Recent Canning Updates**

Canning equipment has changed over the years, becoming more high tech and therefore more efficient at processing foods. In addition to the equipment becoming more advanced, there have also been many scientific improvements, making canning safer when the proper steps are taken. For example, many people used to sterilize their jars before pressure canning. While this is still okay to do, it is not necessary as science has shown that any bacteria in the jars will die when heated to such a high temperature in a pressure canner. Sterilization is an extra step that you just don't need!

Make sure that your food preservation information is all up to date and uses current canning guidelines. Avoid outdated cookbooks and reassess "trusted family methods" to make sure they fit into the most recent criteria for safe canning. When in doubt, check with the US Department of Agriculture's Complete Guide to Home Canning which contains the most recent, up-to-date canning tips.

- **Pick the Best Ingredients**

When choosing food to can, always get the best food possible. You want to use high quality, perfectly ripe produce for canning. You will never end up with a jar of food better than the product itself, so picking good ingredients is important to the taste of your final product. Also, products that past its prime can affect the ability to can it. If strawberries are overripe, your jam may come out too runny. If your tomatoes are past their prime, they may not have a high enough pH level to be processed in a water bath. Pick your ingredients well and you will make successful preserved foods.

- **Clean Everything**

While you may know that your jars and lids need to be washed and sanitized, don't forget about the rest of your tools. Cleaning out your canner before using it is essential, even if you put it away clean. Make sure to wipe your countertop well, making sure there are no crumbs or residue. Wash your produce with clean, cold water and don't forget to wash your hands! The cleaner everything is, the less likely you are to spread bacteria onto your jarred foods

- **Follow Your Recipe**

Use recipes from trusted sources and be sure to follow them to the letter. Changing the amount of one or two ingredients may alter the balance of acidity and could result in unsafe canning (especially when using a water bath canner). Use the ingredients as directed and make very few changes—none if possible.

Adhere to the processing times specified by your recipe. Sometimes the times may seem a little long, but the long processing time is what makes these products safe to store on the shelf. The processing time is the correct amount of time needed to destroy spoilage organisms, mold spores, yeast and pathogens in the jar. So, as you may have guessed, it is extremely important to use the times that are written in your recipe as a hard rule.

- **Cool the Jars**

Be sure that you give your jars 12 hours to cool before testing the seal. If you test the seal too early, it may break as the jar is still warm, making the rubber pliable. Be sure to cool the jars away from a window or fan as even a slight breeze may cause the hot jars to crack. Once cool, remove the metal band, clean it and save it for your next canning project.

- **Don't Risk It**

If you suspect that the food you have canned is bad, don't try to eat it, just toss it! Each time you open a jar of canned food, inspect it and check for the following:

1. Is the lid bulging, swollen, or leaking at all?
2. If the jar cracked or damaged?
3. Does the jar foam when opened?
4. Is the food inside discolored or moldy?
5. Does the food smell bad?

If you notice any of these warning signs in a food that you have canned, throw it away. Do not taste it to check if it is good. It is not worth risking your health to try the food after seeing one of the above signs.

Luckily, it is fairly easy to spot a jar of food that has gone bad. Home-canned food can spoil for many reasons. A dent in the lid, a small crack in the jar, an improper seal, or not enough processing time are all common errors that may cause canned foods to go bad. Follow the exact canning directions and hopefully, you will never get a bad jar of food!

Chapter 12: Canning Do's and Don'ts

Canning is relatively simple but when not done properly, it can result in disastrous consequences. For you to truly be a master on this very important skill, let me provide you with some canning dos and don'ts that you'll surely find helpful.

1. Be Organized

Did you notice that in both water bath and pressure canning methods above studying the recipe is always the first step? This is because knowing what to do keeps you organized. You have to be organized when preserving food since it could help your work go smoothly and canning should be done as quickly as possible.

2. Spices and seasoning only as specified

Do you know that spices and seasoning are usually high in bacteria? Having too many seasonings and spices on your food beyond what was required in the recipe could be unsafe.

3. Overripe fruits and vegetables are a no-no

I have mentioned this before but let me just reiterate this for you, canning can increase the life of the food but it certainly couldn't increase its quality. Canning overripe fruits may become worse in storage.

4. No butter and fat ever

You should not put these two in your home canned products as they do not store well. Adding them to your product will only decrease the food's life. In addition, butter and fat slows heat transfer during the processing time which can result to an unsafe preserve.

5. You can go smaller but not bigger

When it comes to the size of jar you should use, if you can't stick to the jar size on the recipe, then you should pick up a smaller jar than getting a bigger one since this can result in an unsafe product.

6. The higher the altitude = longer processing time

In high altitudes, the boiling point is of lower altitude. This is why you have to increase the processing time to compensate for the lower temperatures at an altitude above 1000 feet.

7. Hot and cold do not go well together

Indeed, hot and cold do not go well together especially when it comes to jars. Abrupt changes in temperature would certainly result in breakage so here are things you should remember: if the food will be hot when placed in the jar, your jar should be preheated and the water in the canner should already be heated to. If the food is cold, do not preheat the jars, just sterilize them. Also, put the jars before turning on the heat on the canner so that the water and the food can be heated together.

8. Safety first before removing jars

After the processing time, jars will sure to be hot in both the water bath and the pressure canning method so you have to make sure to handle them carefully. You can use a footstool to avoid tiptoeing while removing the jars because that could be dangerous!

9. Patience on seals

After removing the jars from the rack and putting them on a paper towel, avoid moving them or you will be interrupting its sealing process. Just leave them be or else put the jars in a place where it wouldn't be disturbed the moment you take them out of the canner.

10. Write the details down meticulously

I'm just talking about the labels on the jars. Remember to always attach a label to each jar and write down the recipe and the production date. This is the best way to keep track of the life span of the food.

To be truly a master of something, you have to work hard on it too. Knowledge of the steps in canning and preserving plus the additional tips I mentioned would not be enough to create a canning master in you. You have to work hard on it too. As always, practice is the key!

Chapter 13: Some Other Food Preservation Techniques

The Milling Technique

The ancient humans found out that by crushing different berries and wheat kernels by placing them in between two pieces of rocks they can get flour, which can be used in a variety of different forms. Since that time grinding flour with the help of various techniques has been part of human civilization.

Milling is used as the easiest way of getting the fullest nutrient content from wheat flour. This method is the demand for modern day as the shelf life of flour needs to be increased as food is supplied from one part of the world to the other. For this reason, the removal of all sorts of grain bran traces and germs is highly essential. Milling as a procedure will enable the user to get the required amount of flour every time so that it can be consumed within a time period of 72 hours.

- **Why go for milling:**

The flour grains consist of around 90% of minerals, vitamins, and protein which are needed by the human body. But in the case of commercially milled flour, the quantity of these nutrients is largely reduced because of artificial additives and processing.

The whole grain comprises of three major parts, two being the germ and the bran. These two hold all of the minerals, vitamins, and proteins. On the other hand, when milled, the oils present in the germ and bran starts oxidizing. So eventually, the flour turns rancid within a period of 72 hours. So the commercial packaging of flour removes all bran and of germ and thus all the connected nutrients, which elongates the shelf life. In Commercially processed flour you will get only the third ingredient of the grain, called endosperm. It is the starchy center, which is white in color and no useful nutrients are present in it.

Methods Applied

If you are also curious about the quality of food you eat and especially the most frequently used eatable, i.e. flour. You need to be curious about this method of food processing.

Various methods of milling are applied, some of which include:

- **Manual Milling**

This allows manual milling of Grain, in which a mill that is operated by hand is applied. Although time-consuming yet this method is quite cost-friendly.

- **Electric Milling**

As compared to manual method electric milling is fast in which mill is supplied with a power connection. If you have to mill large quantities of flour, then this method is the most suitable one.

- **Motorized Milling**

Flour can also be milled in a way that is partially supported by the machines. In this method, the mill is connected to an electric or gas motor along with a pulley system. This method is faster than manual milling but slower than the electric milling process.

The equipment used for various types of mills is as follows:

1. In the case of the stone mill is a set of two grinding stones that are circular in shape. One stein is kept stationary while the other one is moved against it.

2. In the case of burr mill, the grinding wheels of the wheel are made up of steel with tiny burrs extending from the sides.

3. In the case of impact mill, the major assembly is just like the stone mill but various rows of blades are used to circular rows.

Chapter 14: FAQ'S On Canning & Preserving Foods

This book has tried to cover all areas that a beginner or newbie in canning and preserving food would want to know. Nevertheless, there may still be some questions that are hanging in your mind. Here are the most frequently asked questions and their answers regarding canning and preserving foods.

As an interested beginner who would like to take this skill into a higher level, is there a canning class or course that one can take?

Anybody can preserve or can foods without formal education. For those who would like to have advanced canning skills, canning classes are oftentimes offered in some grocery stores, kitchen stores, cooking schools, community centers, and sometimes, even in libraries. You could also search online for correspondence that offers this course. Be careful with blogs or articles that teach canning techniques. Some of these articles may contain ideas or suggestions that go contrary to the recommendations of USDA. If in doubt, refer to the USDA manual or contact an authorized person.

What is the shelf life of canned food?

Properly sealed canned and preserved foods placed in a cool, dry place, with no signs of spoilage inside and out, are considered safe to consume for at least a year. However, canned foods stored near a furnace, in indirect sunlight, a range or anywhere warm can decrease shelf life. It would be safe to consume within a few weeks until a couple of months only. Placing the jars or cans in damp areas may corrode cans and this can cause leakage, causing the food to be contaminated and unsafe to eat.

One of the recipes included pectin as an ingredient in making jams. If a person does not like to use pectin, can he or she omit that ingredient?

Emphasis on the importance of complying with the recipes has been stressed over and over again throughout this book. Do not modify, lessen, remove, or add anything to the recipe if you want to have a perfect outcome. There are many reliable recipes that you can find that do not use pectin. Use these instead rather than trying to change the recipe.

Can you process two layers of jars at one time?

Yes, this can be done. The jars at the upper layer would enjoy the same benefits as those in the bottom. The temperature is equally distributed making it safe for all jars, whether in the upper and lower layer. Just make sure that you place a wire rack between the layers to allow the circulation of water and steam around the jars. Also, when using bath-water canning method, make sure that the water is up to one inch above the tops of the jars in the upper layer. If you are using a pressure canner, the water should be 2 to 3 inches from the bottom. As always, comply with the processing time and required temperature.

During processing, some liquid of the contents were lost. What should be done about it?

If the liquid loss is minimal, there is nothing to worry about. The food will not spoil and the seal will not be affected. It may cause slight discoloration of the food, however, but that's about it. However, if the liquid loss is at least half of the original amount, then the most that you can do is to refrigerate it and consume within 2 to 3 days.

What is kettle canning and is this safe to use?

In this method, the foods to be preserved are cooked in an ordinary household kettle. After that, the foods are placed into hot jars, covered, and sealed. You would notice that no processing is done in this method. In addition, the temperature when using the kettle canning method is not high enough to eliminate the harmful bacteria that may be in the food. Also, during the transfer of food from the kettle to the jars, microorganisms can enter the food and cause spoilage and worse, food poisoning, later on. Therefore, the safety of food is not guaranteed. The kettle canning method is not included in the recommendation of USDA with regards to canning.

Why do some jars break during canning?

There are many reasons breakage occurs during the process of canning. Here are five reasons:

1. The glass of the jar is not tempered. A tempered or toughened glass underwent a process that increased its strength and ability to withstand heat compared to normal glass. Before buying commercial food jars, make sure that they are manufactured for home canning.

2. Another reason is using jars with hairline cracks. These cracks are so thin that they can be missed or overlooked. Such jars would not be able to stand the extreme heat during processing time.

3. Not placing a wire rack on the bottom of the pot or canner could also cause the jars to break.

4. Putting newly cooked food into cold jars. The difference in the temperature between the food and the jars could lead to breakage. That is why it is advised that the jars should be maintained on a hot temperature before filling them with hot food.

5. Jars with unheated or raw food placed directly into boiling water can also break because of the sudden change in temperature. It is better to use hot water first and let it achieve boiling point after several minutes.

An article said that a jam or jelly with molds could still be used. Simply remove or scoop out the parts with molds. The rest would still be okay for consumption. Is this true?

Molds can cause an increase in the pH of the food. For instance, if the canned food is high acid, then because of the raised pH, it could become low acid. This places the preserved food into the risk of having botulism and other bacterial growth. Therefore, all canned foods with molds should be disposed of properly. Follow the proper waste disposal for spoiled canned food.

Can canning be done for those people with special diets?

Some people, because of their medical conditions, would not be allowed to consume some of the canned foods because of some ingredients like sugar and salt. Sugar is discouraged among Diabetic people due to the effect of increased blood sugar with the intake of simple sugar.

On the other hand, salts are always restricted among people with cardiovascular disorders as this can cause increased high blood pressure as more body water is retained because of salts. Still, canning foods can be done for these people even in the absence of salt or sugar. However, the color, texture, flavor of these canned foods will differ from those with sugar or salt in them, as expected. Other people find these special diet canned foods to be less acceptable and less appealing.

You can preserve and can regular fruits even without sugar. The key is selecting firm, fully ripe (but not overripe) fruits of the best quality. In place of sugar syrup, you can use unsweetened fruit juice or plain water. Another technique is to blend some of the same fruits to be canned. This will serve as the syrup or juice of the canned food. Pour the blended fruits into the jar and then add the solid fruits. To make this more palatable, you can add sugar substitutes when serving.

To can vegetables, meats, seafood, or tomatoes without salt, proceed with the regular canning minus the salt. This method is allowed, as salts are not considered as preservatives, hence the safety of food is still guaranteed even in the absence of salt. Salt substitutes can be offered upon serving to make the preserved food taste better.

What is the future of canning and preserving foods?

The trend all over the world right now is towards healthy food and lifestyle. You can see everything "organic" from cosmetics, hair products, food, baby products, and even processed foods. People prefer "fresh" than canned or commercially prepared processed foods.

This is where home canning and preserving fresh fruits, meats, poultry, salsa, vegetables, sauces, and what-have-you enter the picture. This is a combination of being healthy and modern, rolled into one. It meets the requirements of being healthy and at the same time, lasting longer on the shelf or pantry. It is ready to eat, answering the need for convenience and saving precious time.

More and more people are going into canning and preserving food. The threat of not having enough good food to eat in the future due to excessive wasting and unnecessary throwing of food today has found its solution in canning.

Final words on canning and preserving foods

Canning is not only easy, fun, profitable, helpful (both physically and financially) but it is also Earth-friendly. This generation has been blessed with abundance in everything, most especially in the production of food. That is no excuse to be unwise and thoughtless. Make use of excess resources and learn how to preserve and prolong their life spans, rather than just throw them away. Can and preserve food today. This is a good thing to do.

Conclusion

After reading all of this you might be feeling a little overwhelmed. Don't panic, this is natural. Do not let a large amount of information phase you. This book was not written to scare you or make you feel incompetent. No. If anything, this book was written to help you navigate through the challenges home canning may throw in your direction.

Canning your own food is a deeply satisfying activity. When you take a look at your canned foods and you realize that you were able to do it on your own, it will fuel the motivation you need to turn this into a regular habit. If you choose to can your own food on a regular basis, you will notice a decline in the amount of money you use to buy produce and other canned foods. Home canning will also influence your eating habits in a positive way. The foods you will be preserved will be far healthier than the preserved foods that are sold in supermarkets.

Once you get the hang of canning your own food, you will be unstoppable! I will not lie to you and tell you that everything will be easy – especially the first couple of times. You will make a couple of mistakes and you might make a mess of your kitchen too. This is expected – you are a beginner after all.

As time goes by, though, the number of mistakes you make will decrease, and eventually, you won't need this guide to assist you. You will be able to come up with creative recipes of your own! This all has to start with the first steps, the first steps being you arr giving this a chance.

If you aren't feeling confident in your abilities, try out the easiest water bath canning recipe in this book. You can also find a number of safe and

USDA approved recipes online. There are a number of forums dedicated to offering support to home canning beginners.

Don't let your fears stop you from trying out this great method of preserving your own food. It is a highly rewarding experience that is capable of benefitting you for years to come.

You won't regret trying it out.

Thank you again for downloading this book!

I hope this book was able to help you know the basics of food canning and preservation. I hope that this book was able to clearly explain the different concepts and rules when it comes to canning and preserving food. I also hope that you'll be able to follow all the instructions indicated in this book.

The next step is to apply all the things that you have learned from this book. Remember that knowledge without application is useless. Look for canning and preservation recipes online or from different books and start doing them yourself. Just see to it that you will always take into consideration the reminders, especially the fact that you first have to understand the method that you are going to carry out before you start doing anything.

Dehydrating Food

The Beginner's Guide to Dehydrating Vegetables, Fruits, Meat, and Other Foods at Home with Easy Recipes

Lydia Reed

Introduction

With the sun as an abundant energy source, drying is one of the oldest ways humans have preserved food. When properly processed, dried fruits and vegetables lose 10-15% of their water content, which concentrates the sugars left behind in the plant. Remember that microorganisms cannot grow in environments that are saturated in sugar, making drying one of the easiest, most reliable methods of preservation. As foods dry, they become lighter, making them convenient snacks for in between meals, out on a hike, or in the kids' lunches. They save tons of space in the pantry and are great additions to recipes. Fruits like apples and peaches can be dried as well as vegetables like onions, celery, peppers, garlic, and herbs.

Dried foods are also the most nutritious of all of the preservation methods highlighted in this book, typically losing no more than 3-5% of their original nutritional value. Because they are made out of whole fruits and vegetables, dried foods are packed with fiber and low in fat.

Dehydrators perform a simple operation: A fan and motor circulate heated air through the machine, which results in the removal of moisture from the food on the dehydrator trays. Foods with high water content, such as bell peppers, take longer to dehydrate than foods with a lower water content, such as kale. Likewise, food with a high density, such as a large bean, will take longer to dry than food with a lower density, such as rice.

To get the best results when dehydrating the recipes in this book, pay close attention to the directions for prepping the vegetables. If the recipe calls for cutting the vegetables into ½-inch dice, be sure to cut them to that size so they will dehydrate at the same rate as the rest of the recipe. If you are uncertain what ½-inch dice looks like, measure and cut a piece to that size and set it aside as a guide. Cutting larger pieces than is called for is easy to do by accident, and that will affect how the recipe itself turns out, the drying time, and the consistency of the food.

When food comes out of the dehydrator, it looks vastly different from its original state. Hummus and soups can look as cracked and parched as a desert floor. Food can come off the trays in thin sheets, which you can break into smaller pieces. Properly dried pieces of fruit bend but don't break, and they do not feel moist when you squeeze them. Other foods—vegetables, grains, and legumes—should be hard and dry.

It is possible to burn food in a dehydrator, so pay attention to both the temperature and timing recommendations given in the recipes. Also, when you're learning how to dehydrate food, be sure to check the food every few hours. You may need to rotate the trays to ensure that the food dries evenly, and if you find that part of your recipe is dry before the rest, remove that part and store it while the rest of the recipe continues to dry. There is often one ingredient in each recipe that takes longer to dry than the rest, and that ingredient will be called out in the recipe as the barometer for when the food is dry. In the <u>Red Curry Vegetable Stir-Fry</u>, for example, that ingredient is the red bell pepper, which has a very high-water content.

The amount of food that will fit on a dehydrator tray varies somewhat, based on viscosity or density, so some experimentation will be required. Start with about one cup of food and spread it out evenly, to about ½ inch from the edge of the tray. You should have an even, thin layer of food, with no significantly larger chunks. If there is still room on the tray once the food is spread out, you can add a bit more until the entire tray surface is full.

DRYING FOOD

Dehydration is a simple and ancient means of preserving food. Drying food was a way to save and store harvests of fruit, grains, and vegetables. Laying out food on mats to dry under the sun morphed into hand-built dehydrator boxes with mesh trays. Once ovens with reliably consistent temperatures existed, food was dried on oven trays. Some people still use ovens for dehydration, and if your oven has a minimum temperature setting of lower than 170°F and convection air, you may be able to use it for dehydrating food. Now we have the convenience of electric dehydrators that offer several improvements over other methods. Different types of foods require specific temperatures for food safety and the most efficient drying times. Circulating air prompts faster drying times as well.

Chapter 1: Dehydrating Basics

Dehydrating Methods

You can get started drying using items you probably already have in your kitchen.

The following items are essential to the drying process:

- **Food.**

- **A source of heat.**

- **Trays or racks to dry the food on.**

The trays should be slotted wood or mesh trays. Avoid using solid trays because they block air from circulating all the way around the food. In a pinch, you can cover a wood frame with cheesecloth and use it as a drying rack.

CONTAINERS TO STORE THE FOOD IN:

That's it. That's all you need to get started drying. There are other items you can use to make life easier on yourself, but the above items are the only absolute necessities.

You want to avoid trays made from the following materials because they can add harmful substances to your food during the drying process:

- **Fiberglass.**
- **Vinyl.**
- **Aluminum.**
- **Copper.**
- **Plastic.**
- **Galvanized metal.**

The following items aren't required, but will make life easier on you:

- **A commercial food dehydrator.**
- **A fan.**
- **A blancher.**
- **A sulfur box.**
- **A scale.**
- **A thermometer.**

Now that we've established the items you need and the items you can buy to make life easier, let's take a look at the various methods used to dehydrate food.

Use a fan to circulate fresh air into the area where the food is drying.

1. Using Your Oven

If you have an oven (and who doesn't?), you have a tool you can use to dry foods.

It isn't the best choice when it comes to drying, but it'll work in a pinch. The upside to using this method is it's one of the fastest methods of drying food. The downside is you can easily burn or scorch the food you're drying because it's difficult to keep the heat as low as you need it. You can only dry small amounts of food in a normal kitchen oven. If you're planning on drying large amounts of food, buy a dehydrator and save yourself a lot of work.

You need to keep your oven temperature somewhere between 140 and 160 degrees F. To check oven temps, place an oven thermometer on the top rack and leave it there so you can monitor it. The temperature needs to be checked every 15 minutes to make sure it isn't getting too hot.

Place the food in a single layer on the drying trays. You can usually fit a couple pounds of food on each tray. Since most ovens have two racks, you're only going to be able to dry around 4 pounds of food at a time.

Here's a little trick you can use to fit more food in the oven: Place a couple 1 ½-inch tall wood blocks on the bottom tray and set the next drying tray on the blocks. Then add a couple more blocks to the second tray and place another tray on it. You can fit up to four racks in your oven using this method, which will effectively double the amount of food you're able to dry at once. Since you're not heating the oven up too hot, you don't have to worry about scorching or burning the wood.

You need to prop the door open so there's a gap of 2 to 6 inches during the drying process. If you have a fan, set it up so it's blowing air into the oven through this gap. You need to keep the air inside moving so the oven doesn't fill full of humid air.

2. Set your oven at its lowest temperature

If you have a gas oven, you may be able to get away with just using the heat from the pilot light. Monitor the temperature to ensure it stays above 140 degrees F and below 160 degrees F.

The top rack is going to be a little cooler than the bottom rack. Additionally, the air isn't going to be the same temperature in the front of the oven as it is in the back, especially if you're using a fan to circulate air. For this reason, it's important to rotate the trays every 20 to 30 minutes. Rotate the top trays to the bottom and flip the trays around so the food that was in the front is now in the back. You're also going to want to periodically flip your food over or stir it on the tray because the side of the food that's facing down will dry at a slower rate than the side that's facing up.

I've already mentioned the temperature you need to keep your food at a couple times, but it's important enough that I'm going to mention it again. It's tough to keep your temperature between 140 and 160 degrees F in a conventional oven, so you need to monitor it closely. Too low of a temperature and your food won't dry out. Too high and you're cooking your food instead of drying it.

If you have a toaster oven, it can be used to dry small amounts of food, leaving your oven open for other tasks. I wouldn't run out and by one just for dehydrating foods, because you can get a dedicated dehydrator for close to the same price.

The process used to dry foods in a toaster oven is same as with a conventional oven. Place the food on a tray and put it in your toaster oven. Set the oven on its lowest setting and prop open the door. If you have a fan, use it to circulate new air into the oven.

Since this sort of oven is smaller than a conventional oven, it's going to dehydrate the food you're drying faster than the larger oven. Make sure you watch it closely and soon you'll have a small batch of dried foods.

Here's a quick tip you won't see in too many other books about drying: Open the door of your oven every few hours to let out all the damp air trapped inside. Sure, it will cause the temperature to drop inside, but it will let all the moist air inside escape, replacing it with dry air. The hit you take in temperature is temporary and it's worth it to fill the oven with fresh air.

If you only dry occasionally, your oven will do the trick nicely.

3.   Sun-Drying

A Sun-drying food is the oldest method used to dehydrate foods, predating ovens by thousands of years. This method is all-natural and doesn't require use of electricity or gas (to preserve the food or store it). All you need is a nice, sunny day or two (or 5) in a row and you can use the power of the sun to dry your food.

In warmer climates, you can dry food using this method year-round. In cooler places or in areas where there's typically a lot of cloud cover, there may only be a handful of days a year this method can be used.

You need dry, clear weather with temperatures of at least 90 to 100 degrees F to sun-dry food.

If you live in an area where it's typically cloudy or there's a lot of moisture in the air, you're probably better off using one of the other methods of dehydrating. It's OK to move foods you've started sun-drying in and finishing the process in the oven or a dehydrator if it looks like inclement weather is on its way.

To sun-dry your foods, spread a layer out on a wood frame covered in cheesecloth. If you're worried about bugs or other animals getting to your food, you can place a layer of cheesecloth over the top of your food as well. Turn your foods regularly to assure even drying or the side left exposed to the sun will dry at a faster clip.

Alternatively, you can run a piece of string through your food items and hang them out to dry. Items like meat can be hung from hooks.

Spread food out in a single layer with at least a couple millimeters space between each piece so air can flow around it. Set the tray out in an area that gets sun for most of the day and has good circulation. Now, all you have to do is leave it there until the food is dry.

Leave the food out during the heat of the day, and then move it inside during the evening and night hours.

This accomplishes two things. It prevents the food from rehydrating due to condensation and it keeps the critters away. Animals enjoy dehydrated foods as much as you do and have been known to raid backyards at night. You don't want all of your hard work to be wasted at the hands of a marauding deer or raccoon.

Flip the food partway through each day. The bottom side gets less air and sun and will lose less moisture. Flip the food you're cooking over regularly so both side get equal amounts of sun.

There's no set time you need to leave food out to dry. All times shown in books and on the Internet are approximations of what it takes under "normal" conditions.

What exactly constitutes normal conditions is anyone's guess. What's normal in one place would be out of the ordinary somewhere else. That's probably why there's such variation in the dry times in different literature. I've tried to provide ranges in this book, but even the ranges can be off. The only way to make sure you dry your food correctly is to keep a close eye on it. When it gets close to the bottom end of the range, check it periodically.

The drying time varies based on the heat applied to the food, the humidity and the circulation of air in the area you're doing the drying. The hotter it is the faster food is going to lose moisture. The more humidity there is the slower moisture is going to be absorbed.

If you live in an area with a lot of vehicle traffic or high pollution levels, you shouldn't air-dry your food outside. Pollution particles can land on your food and contaminate it. Over time, the particulates you're eating can build up in your system and make you sick.

Looks like a great day for drying.

Dehydrating Equipment

Dehydration is mostly about prep work, so having the appropriate tools will make your job easier. Make sure you have the following tools on hand.

1. **Baking sheet:** If you don't already have one, a good-quality baking sheet that disperses heat properly and doesn't buckle under high heat is a great addition to your kitchen. Use it for roasting vegetables and fish.

2. **Blender:** Blenders are great for making purées for sauces, soups, and fruit leather. A food processor or immersion blender also works for this purpose.

3. **Four-cup measuring pitcher:** These pitchers are good for measuring liquids and for measuring the yield of dehydrated foods (if you don't have a kitchen scale).

4. **Kitchen knife:** Aside from the dehydrator itself, a kitchen knife is the most important tool for dehydrating. A good knife will make your prep work much easier. Perhaps you already have a favorite knife one that keeps a good edge, has a straight blade, and is comfortable to hold for extended periods. Good knives don't need to be expensive. In our kitchen we use the same knives many culinary schools offer; they are inexpensive but great tools for the job.

5. **Kitchen scale:** An inexpensive digital scale is very useful for measuring ingredients with precision and is also helpful for measuring and portioning the completed and dehydrated meals.

6. **Parchment paper:** Line baking sheets with parchment paper to prevent food from sticking to the pan. It also makes for easy cleanup.

Chapter 2: How to Dehydrate

Preparing Fruits for Dehydratio

Most dehydrating machines, no matter which brand or model you choose, are user-friendly. The first step in preparing fruits for the dehydration machine is selecting high-quality fruits.

Fruit should be fresh and at the peak of ripeness. Once you pick or purchase your produce, thoroughly wash it and discard any bruised or damaged pieces. Fruits may need to be peeled, cored or pitted, depending on the particular fruit you are handling.

After fruit has been peeled and sliced, it is advisable to apply a pre-treatment to maintain the color and freshness of the produce. Once certain fruits, such as apples, pears and peaches are sliced, their exposure to air initiates a chemical process called oxidation that results in discolored flesh. Using an antioxidant will temporarily halt the enzyme action and prevent further damage to the texture, flavor and appearance of the fruit. To make this solution, combine a small amount of ascorbic acid (1-2 tsp.) with one cup of water and coat the fruit evenly with the liquid.

Preparing Vegetables for Dehydration

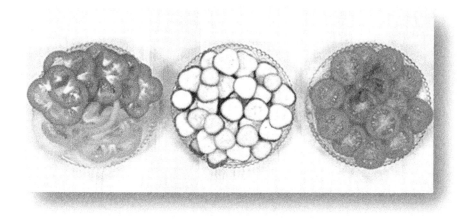

When preparing your vegetables for dehydration, be sure to select high-quality, unblemished vegetables.

Particularly for certain vegetables such as root vegetables and potatoes, make sure they are thoroughly scrubbed and cleaned prior to dehydration. Similar to fruits, vegetables should be sliced thinly and uniformly for the best results.

Nearly all vegetables should be blanched first. Blanching vegetables halts enzyme action and thereby preserves the color and flavor of the food over time. Because some nutrients may be lost during the blanching process, place the vegetables in boiling water only for the required length of time.

After the vegetables are submerged in ice cold water, carefully dry the foods prior to placing them on trays. Note that a small number of vegetables, like mushrooms and onions, do not need to be blanched prior to dehydration.

Preparing Meat for Dehydration

Dehydrated meats are delicious and simple to prepare, but do warrant special handling instructions. Only lean meats in excellent condition should be utilized for making jerky. When using ground meat for jerky, it should be at least 93% lean.

All other meat should have its fat thoroughly trimmed prior to slicing.

You might consider applying a marinade beforehand to flavor the meat. If so, keep marinated meats in the refrigerator or freezer before placing them in the dehydrator. After removing the meat from the refrigerator, blot its surface thoroughly to remove excess moisture and place on dehydrator trays. As always, raw meat should be kept away from other foods, and all surfaces and utensils that come into contact with raw meat should be thoroughly cleaned.

After using the dehydrator, experts recommend heating dried meat strips for ten minutes in a 275° F oven or for a longer time at a lower temperature. This additional step reduces any residual chance of contamination by eliminating pathogens, and also produces the most traditional style of jerky with respect to taste and texture.

Preparing Grains, Nuts, Beans and Seeds for Dehydration

Nuts, seeds, beans and grains can all be dehydrated using a similar two-step process. First, these foods must be soaked in a water solution. Soaking deactivates anti-nutrients, stimulates nutrients such as iron, potassium and magnesium, and is beneficial to your digestive system. Soak nuts or seeds in a salt brine solution for 12-18 hours. Add ½ tsp. high-quality sea salt for every cup of water. Since wet nuts and seeds are not appealing to most people, you can place the nuts in the dehydrator to create a delicious, crunchy, ready to eat snack. After soaking for the recommended time, drain the water and proceed with instructions for your dehydrating machine.

Using Your Dehydrator Machine

Once the fruits, vegetables, herbs, meat, nuts or grains have been prepped, spread them in thin layers without overlapping on the drying trays. Turn on the dehydrating machine and set the temperature. Drying times vary depending on the dehydrator model you own and the food you are dehydrating. Most dehydrators contain guides that provide recommended temperatures and times for dehydrating specific foods.
In general, it is recommended that fruits and vegetables be dried at 130°-140° F. Meats and fish should be dehydrated at the highest temperature setting on your machine, which is typically between 145°-155° F. When

dehydrating meats, it is necessary to use dehydrator models with adjustable temperature controls to ensure a product that is safe for consumption. Dried herbs require a temperature not exceeding 90° F, as aromatic oils in herbs are sensitive to high heat. Nuts, seeds and grains, which also have a high oil content, dry optimally at 90°-100° F.

Determining Food Readiness

Foods should always be tested for adequate dehydration before removal. Many factors determine the length of time necessary to dehydrate foods, such as the temperature, humidity, type of food, amount of food on the tray, size of the food pieces, and total quantity of food in the machine.

In general, meats should be dehydrated to 20% moisture content, fruits to 10% and vegetables to about 5%. You can analyze the appearance and texture of foods for signs of readiness. It is important to test only a few pieces at a time and allow them to cool before determining whether they are ready.

Checking food for readiness is largely a matter of assessing its structure. Fruits should be pliable, but not totally brittle. Test fruits by cutting them in half; if you cannot squeeze out any moisture, then the fruit are fully dehydrated. Vegetables, however, should be brittle when they are done. Test vegetables by hitting them with a hammer to see if they shatter.

Most fully dehydrated vegetables should break into pieces. Certain vegetables, however, will retain a pliable and leathery texture upon complete dehydration. These include mushrooms, green peppers and squash. To test jerky, bend one piece and see how pliable it is. The meat should bend, but not snap completely like a dry stick. The jerky should present as dark brown to black in color once it is fully dehydrated. Herbs are considered dried when they crumble easily. The stems of the herb should bend and break with little effort.

Chapter 3: Fruits and Nuts

Drying Fruit

Drying fruit is a delicious and easy way to preserve a bountiful harvest. It's a great way to ensure fruit lasts longer and is more convenient to pack away and to store.

Dried fruit is a great snack, but is best when consumed in moderation. Dried fruits are both tasty and nutritious, but you have to be careful not to eat too much because they can be high in calories and tend to contain a lot of sugar. While some of the nutrients may be lost during processing and drying, the calories and sugar remain the same.

While dried vegetables and herbs are usually consumed as part of another dish they've been added to in order to add flavor, dried fruits are usually consumed on their own. If you like a certain type of fruit, there's a pretty good chance you're going to like the dried version of it as well. The flavor is usually intensified and the dried fruit will usually be sweeter than its fresh counterpart.

The same drying methods that work for vegetables also work for fruit. Solar drying, oven drying and electric dehydration are all viable fruit drying methods. Fruits are better-suited to solar drying because the acid and sugar content makes them less likely to go bad during the extended periods of time required for solar drying. For this reason, fruit can be dried when temperatures outside are slightly lower than what's required to dry vegetables.

The Sugar Content of Dried Fruit

There's no getting around the fact that dried fruits have more sugar per ounce than regular fruit. This is because the dehydration process removes most of the water from the fruit, but has a negligible effect on the sugar. Dried fruit is significantly smaller than regular fruit of the same type, but the sugar found in a piece of dried fruit is pretty much equal to the sugar found in a piece of undried fruit.

One cup of regular apple slices contains 13 to 15 grams of sugar. A cup of dried apples contains nearly 50 grams of sugar. Dried apples have more than three times the sugar by volume as regular apples. Apples aren't the fruit to experience this phenomenon. The following chart lists some of the usual dried fruits and compares the sugar content between the dried and the raw versions of the fruit:

Type of Fruit

- Sugar in 1 Cup of Raw Fruit
- Sugar in 1 Cup of Dried Fruit

Apples

- 13 to 15 grams
- 45 to 50 grams

Apricots

- 15 grams
- 70 grams

Bananas

- 25 to 30 grams
- 45 to 50 grams

Blueberries

- 15 grams
- 80 to 90 grams

Cherries

- 17 to 20 grams
- 70 to 80 grams

Cranberries

- 4 grams

Figs

- 10 grams
- 70 grams

Grapes/Raisins

- 15 grams
- 100 grams

Kiwi

- 15 grams
- 70 grams

Mangoes

- 25 grams
- 90 to 100 grams

Melon

- 10 grams
- 60 to 70 grams

Papaya

- 10 grams
- 70 to 80 grams

Peaches

- 15 grams
- 70 grams

Pears

- 15 grams
- 110 grams

Pineapple

- 16 grams
- 48 grams

Plums/Prunes

- 15 grams
- 65 grams

Strawberries

- 5 to 7 grams

- 60 to 70 grams

Accurate data on the sugar content of dried cranberries isn't available because dried cranberries are usually sweetened. The sweetened version of dried cranberries contains 70 to 80 grams of sugar per cup.

Pretreating Fruit

Pretreatment helps prevent fruit from darkening. Fruits like apples and bananas will quickly start to brown and start to deteriorate as soon as they're exposed to air. Without pretreatment, fruits that darken due to enzymatic reactions will continue to darken during the drying process and even after drying is complete.

Sulfur or a sulfite dip can be used to stop the enzymatic reaction that causes fruit to brown and degrade. There are some dangers associated with use of sulfites, as they are passed into the food being dried in amounts high enough to cause problems in those sensitive to sulfites. Asthmatics tend to be particularly sensitive to sulfites and there have been a small number of deaths attributed to the use of sulfites in foods. The risk is slim, but it is there and I want to make sure you know about it in advance.

Sulfuring isn't required for most fruit that will be consumed shortly after drying, but it's one of the better methods for preserving food over the long term. Dried foods can also be frozen to slow enzymatic actions. This might be the better option if you have an at-risk person in your home.

There are two common methods of sulfuring fruits. The traditional method involves placing fruit into a wooden box and burning sulfur in the box to allow the smoke to permeate the fruit. Sulfur gas is toxic in larger amounts, making this method the more dangerous of the two. It isn't recommended you use this method, as the risks outweigh the potential benefits.

The second method involves creating a sulfite dip using sodium bisulfite or sodium sulfite. Only use food grade or Reagent grade sulfites. Add a teaspoon of sodium sulfite to 4 cups of water and stir it in. Prepare the fruit and let it soak in the sulfite solution for 5 to 15 minutes. Rinse the food off and pat it dry before dehydrating it.

An even safer, albeit not as long-lived, method of pretreating fruits is to dip them in an ascorbic acid treatment. Ascorbic acid, which is vitamin C in powdered form, prevents browning, but doesn't last as long as sulfuring does. You can purchase it at most grocery stores and some drugstores. Add 2 teaspoons of ascorbic acid to 4 cups of water and soak the fruit in it for 5 minutes. Alternatively, you can use fruit juice like lemon, orange or pineapple juice that is high in vitamin C.

Blanching is another option that may help prevent fruit from browning. It isn't used as extensively as it is with vegetables, but there are a handful of fruits that can be blanched. Steam blanching is the most popular blanching technique. Use a double broiler to steam blanch fruit and make sure the fruit doesn't touch the water.

A solution of water, corn syrup and sugar can also be used for blanching. Combine equal parts sugar and light corn syrup. Add a few cups of water to the mix and bring it to a boil. Include the fruit to the hot syrup and let it simmer for 10 to 15 minutes. This method of blanching adds a significant amount of sugar to the fruit.

Whole fruit often needs to be checked in boiling water for 30 to 40 seconds. This will cause the skins to split open, which will give the water inside an easy route through which it can escape as it evaporates. Fruits with thick or waxy skins like figs and blueberries are prime candidates for checking. Be sure to immediately dip the fruit in an ice water bath after checking to make sure the cooking process is brought to a halt.

Drying Times for Fruit

Since dried fruit is typically eaten without taking time to rehydrate it, most fruits aren't dried as extensively as vegetables. You'd break your teeth trying to crunch down fruit that's been dried that much. Instead, shoot for 15% to 20% moisture left in the fruit being dried. This will leave it preserved enough to be stored for longer periods of time, but not so dry as to be brittle.

Most dried fruits feel tough and leathery to the touch, but are still soft enough to be pliable. The exceptions to this rule are banana chips and dried watermelon, which are both crisp to the touch.

The times in this book are only estimates and actual drying times can vary greatly from what's here in print due to a number of variables. Dry fruit until all visible moisture is gone and it is no longer tacky and sticky. To test fruit to see if it's dry, wait for the piece(s) you're testing to cool and cut them in half. If you can see moisture or squeeze juice from the fruit, it needs to be dried longer.

Pasteurizing Fruit

If you've sun-dried your fruit or dried your fruit in an open area where it may have come in contact with insects, it's a good idea to pasteurize it to kill off any insects or insect eggs that might be on the fruit. This won't get rid of the eggs, but it will ensure they won't hatch into insects that will eat the food and further contaminate it.

There are two common pasteurization techniques:

- Heating. Bring the fruit to 175 degrees F and keep it there for 20 to 30 minutes. This can be made in a regular oven. Don't use too much heat or cook the food for too long.

- Freezing. Place the food in a freezer bag and let it sit in the freezer for a couple days.

- Either of these pasteurization techniques will kill off insect eggs and make the food safer for long-term storage.

Chapter 4: Fruit Leathers

Fruits and Fruit Leathers

Fruits are natures' candy but without added preservatives. You can dehydrate them in their peak season when they are cheapest and save them to enjoy all year round.

Select only good fruits that are at the peak of their maturity. Get them from the local farmers' market or local farmers to ensure the best quality. Do not go for damaged fruits as it will yield damaged dehydrated products. They shouldn't be too ripe (unless you want to turn them into fruits leather) for they will become too sweet and squishy after drying.

PREPARING, PRE-TREATING AND DRYING FRUITS:

After selection, comes the preparation and dehydration stage. Various fruits have their specific pre-treatments, preparation steps, and drying time. Below are the general guidelines.

1. **Apples**

Remove skin and core, then slice them into the desired size. Blanch for 5 minutes. Treat with ascorbic acid or citric acid to avoid discolouration. Drying time: 12 hours.

2. **Apricots**

Remove the pit and slice them into the desired size. Blanch for 4 minutes and then treat with ascorbic acid or citric acid. Drying time: 8 to 24 hours.

3. **Bananas**

Pick ripe banana without any green part. Peel and slice into circles. Then, treat with ascorbic acid or citric acid. Drying time: 8 to 12 hours.

4. Blueberries, huckleberries and cranberries

Wash them and crack skin. Drying time: 12 to 24 hours.

5. Cherries

Remove stem and pit. Cut into halves, or you can leave whole, in that case, crack their skins. Drying time: 12 to 24 hours.

6. Figs

Use ripe figs only and crack skin. Drying time: 6 to 12 hours.

7. Blackberries, boysenberries, strawberries, raspberries

There's no treatment required for them. Drying time: 12 to 24 hours.

8. Grapes

Slice the grapes in half and de-seed them. If left whole, their skin needs to be cracked. Drying time: 6 to 12 hours.

9. Nectarines and peaches

Pit and cut them in half. Blanch for 3 minutes. Then, treat with ascorbic acid or citric acid. Drying time: 24 to 48 hours.

10. Pineapples

Pick only ripe pineapple. Cut off the thorns and core. Slice them in ¾ inch pieces for dehydration. Drying time: 12 to 24 hours.

11. Plums/Prunes

Leave them whole and crack skin. Drying time: 24 to 48 hours.

12. Tomatoes

Scald and chill. Remove skin and then slice. Drying time: 24 to 48 hours. To ensure complete dryness, pull pieces from different sections of the dehydrator and test by cutting in half and squeezing the fruit. If you see liquid upon pressing, it still needs more time in the dehydrator.

Fruit leather

Fruit leather is not only a tasty treat but also save your fruits from ending into the bin. You can pick your overripe fruits to make fruits leathers. What you need is a blender or food processor to blend the fruits. Cook apples, peaches, nectarines and pears before blending. Others fruits can be blend directly without cooking. Cooking is essential; otherwise, the leathers will be hard and brittle. For adding sweetness in your leathers, never use powdered or granulated sugar, for it will crystallise over time. Instead mix honey, stevia, or corn syrup.

Basic Method

- Blend the fruit well in a blender along with lemon juice and corn starch. Corn starch prevents the leather from cracking, whereas lemon juice boosts the fruit colour along with vitamin C. If you want to increase the flexibility of the leather so can roll it up, add corn syrup while blending. The blended fruits should be flowing smoothly like applesauce. If too thick, add water or fruit juice.

- Line your dehydrator trays with drying sheets (comes with most of the dehydrators) before pouring the blended fruits mixture. If you don't have one, you can go for oven liners.

- Pour the puree onto the prepared trays and spread it evenly with the help of a spatula. Slapping the dehydrator trays for even spreading can also be done. Make sure it is of uniform thickness. Then, dehydrate them until there is no wet spot left, and fruit puree is like the texture of leather.

- When the leather is still warm, you can roll it up in plastic wrap or parchment paper to store it. Or you can also place them flat in an individual zip-lock plastic bag or airtight jars or containers. Make sure to separate each leather with parchment paper inserted in between to keep them from sticking. Store in a cool, dry place; they will keep for up to a year.

Chapter 5: Vegetables

Dehydrating fresh produce entails a little more work. These need to be rinsed, peeled, and sliced into thin layers. Some may need blanching, boiling, coring and/or de-seeding.

Always dehydrate fresh produce in a conventional oven, with temperature set between 49° / 120° and 54° / 130° only. This allows gradual loss of moisture and prevents smaller pieces from burning.

When using the dehydrator, set the machine at lowest heat for delicate vegetables (e.g. leafy vegetables, onions, etc.); and at highest heat for hardier produce (e.g. legumes, root crops, etc.) or those that have thicker cuts.

Use approximately 1½ to 2 pounds per rotation.

- **Artichoke hearts, green peas, freshly shelled, etc.**

1. Blanch with hot water and then dunk into an ice bath immediately to preserve color.

2. Drain well. Pat-dry using paper towels, if needed.

3. Follow recommended steps for oven drying or dehydrating. See: Oven drying: on page 28 and Dehydrating: on page 29. These may take between five to fourteen hours. These are done when these become brittle and wrinkled.

- **Beets, carrots, cassava, daikon (Asian radish,) potatoes, purple carrots, purple yam, sweet potatoes, yam, zucchini.**

  1. Scrub skins well.
  2. Except for the zucchini, parboil (partially boil) veggies until slightly fork-tender (or when you can pierce outer layer with a fork.)
  3. Remove from water and dunk into an ice bath immediately.
  4. When veggies are cool enough to touch, peel, and slice into ⅛-inch thick disks. Drain well. Pat-dry using paper towels, if needed.
  5. Follow recommended steps for oven drying or dehydrating. See: Oven drying: on page 28 and Dehydrating: on page 29. Beets may need three to ten hours of drying. These are done when individual disks feel dry and leathery to the touch. (Important: wear food-safe gloves to prevent beet juice from staining your hands.)

Carrots, potatoes, purple yam, sweet potatoes, and yam may need six to twelve hours. While the zucchini may need five to ten hours of drying. These are done when chips become crispy. Some pieces may have air pockets or browned edges, but these are normal.

- **Broccoli, cauliflower**

1. Slice into bite-sized florets.

2. Blanch with hot water and then dunk into an ice bath immediately to preserve color.

3. Drain well. Pat-dry using paper towels, if needed.

4. Follow recommended steps for oven drying or dehydrating. See: Oven drying: on page 28 and Dehydrating: on page 29. Broccoli may need four to ten hours. Cauliflower may need six to fourteen hours. Veggies are done when edges are brittle, but the meatier parts are somewhat pliable. Deepening or lightening of colors may be expected.

- ## Corn kernels – fresh off the cob, canned

  1. Rinse canned corn kernels; or blanch fresh corn with hot water and then dunk into an ice bath immediately to preserve color.

  2. Drain well. Pat-dry using paper towels, if needed.

  3. Follow recommended steps for oven drying or dehydrating. See: Oven drying: on page 28 and Dehydrating: on page 29. Corn may need six to twelve hours. Corn kernels are done when these feel hard and edges are brittle and almost powdery.

- ## French beans, green beans, haricot beans, snow peas, etc.

  1. Snap ends off and remove strings. Slice these into inch long slivers.

  2. Blanch with hot water and then dunk into an ice bath immediately to preserve color.

  3. Drain well. Pat-dry using paper towels, if needed.

4. Follow recommended steps for oven drying or dehydrating. See: Oven drying: on page 28 and Dehydrating: on page 29. These may take between six to twelve hours. Veggies are done when these become brittle and crumble when pinched. Shrinkage and wrinkling are to be expected.

- ## Herbs

   1. Remove inedible parts of herbs (e.g. roots, tough stems, yellowing leaves, etc.) Slice these into inch long slivers.

   2. Rinse and drain well. Squeeze out and shake off excess moisture.

   3. Leave these out to dry on a baking sheet lined with paper towels for at least an hour prior to use.

   4. Place herbs in single layers on dehydrator trays. Follow recommended steps for dehydrating. See: Dehydrating: on page 29.

Leafy vegetables and blooms, like: baby spinach leaves, basil leaves, beet tops, cabbage, celery, chicory, Chinese cabbage, chives, collard greens, cress, dandelion, fennel leaves, green onions, kale, leeks, mint leaves, mustard greens, napa cabbage, parsley, perilla, plantain blossoms, pumpkin blossoms, squash blossoms, Swiss chard, taro leaves, turnip greens, and vegetable fern.

   1. Rinse and drain blooms / leaves well. Squeeze-dry. Remove tough ribs and stalks.

   2. Leave these out to dry on a baking sheet lined with paper towels for at least an hour prior to use.

   3. Using paper towels, pat each flower or leaf dry.

   4. Tear leaves into more manageable pieces.

5. Place these in single layers on dehydrator trays. Follow recommended steps for dehydrating. See: Dehydrating: on page 29.

- ## Onions and shallots.

  1. Peel and slice onions and shallots into ¼-inch thick slivers.

  2. Add ¼ tsp. of salt and mash these well. Set aside for 10 to 15 minutes.

  3. Rinse and drain well. Squeeze out excess moisture.

  4. Leave these out to dry on a baking sheet lined with paper towels for at least two hours prior to use. Replace paper towels every thirty minutes.

  5. Place onion slivers in single layers on dehydrator trays.

  6. Follow recommended steps for dehydrating. See: Dehydrating:

Vegetable Leathers

Vegetable leathers are essentially dehydrated pureed vegetables. These can be made from raw, partially cooked, or fully cooked vegetables. These recipes require: blender / food processor (or grater,) fine meshed strainer, and an offset spatula.

Cucumber Leather (Raw)

INGREDIENTS:

- ½ pound fresh cucumbers
- 1/16 tsp. sea salt, optional

PREPARATION:

1. Remove cucumber ends. Peel these if you prefer smoother leathers, or leave unpeeled for a chewier texture but scrub skins

well. Remove seeds. Process in blender until relatively smooth. Substitute carrots or zucchini, if desired.

Oven drying:

Additional equipment: aluminum foil, food-grade bag, offset spatula, oven mitts, rimmed baking sheet, silicon mat or parchment paper, tea towel, trivet

1. Preheat oven to 49°C / 120°F. Line baking sheet with aluminum foil. Leave small overhangs at all sides. Place silicon mat on top.

2. Spread pureed cucumber on silicon mat to about ⅛-inch thick using an offset spatula. Season with sea salt, if using.

3. Bake for thirty to sixty minutes (depending on moisture content of vegetable) with the door closed shut. Check for scorching in fifteen minute intervals. If parts of the leather seems to be browning too fast, cover baking sheet with aluminum foil. Continue baking until vegetable leather is set and no longer tacky.

4. Remove baking sheet from oven. Cool completely to room temperature before peeling off vegetable leather. Either roll up the entire vegetable leather, or slice into more manageable squares. Use as needed.

5. To store: place in food-grade bag. Put away at room temperature or inside the fridge. Vegetable leather should be consumed within three days for maximum flavor.

Dehydrating:

Additional equipment: food grade bags, offset spatula, saran wrap

1. Preheat machine to highest setting.

2. Line trays with saran wrap with small overhangs on all sides. This makes it easier to peel off vegetable leather later on.

3. Pour small amount of pureed vegetable on the trays. Spread to about ⅛-inch thick using an offset spatula.

4. Dehydrate for four to six hours. Rotate trays every hour. Vegetable leather is done when this is no longer tacky, but still pliable.

5. Turn off heat. Cool completely to room temperature. Remove vegetable leather from trays. Either leave whole, or slice these into quarters. Use as needed.

6. To store: place in food-grade bag. Take away as much air from the bag before sealing. Store at room temperature, or in the fridge. Consume within three days for maximum flavor.

Vegetable Leather (Partially Cooked)

Use unsalted / unseasoned 15 oz. canned beans, chickpeas, creamed corn, peas, pumpkins, squash, etc. Rinse and drain well.

Process veggies in blender to make a relatively smooth paste. Add a couple of tablespoons of warm water if paste is too chunky or too thick to spread evenly.

If desired, lightly season vegetable leather prior to oven drying or dehydrating.

Oven drying:

Additional equipment: aluminum foil, food-grade bag, offset spatula, oven mitts, rimmed baking sheet, silicon mat or parchment paper, tea towel, trivet

1. Preheat oven to 49°C / 120°F. Line baking sheet with aluminum foil. Leave small overhangs on all sides. Place silicon mat on top.

2. Spread vegetables on silicon mat to about ⅛-inch thick using an offset spatula. Season with sea salt or sugar, if desired.

3. Bake for thirty to sixty minutes with the door closed shut. Check for scorching in fifteen minute intervals.

4. If parts of the leather seems to be browning too fast, cover baking sheet with aluminum foil. Continue baking until vegetable leather is set and no longer tacky.

5. Remove baking sheet from oven. Cool completely to room temperature before peeling off vegetable leather. Either roll up the entire vegetable leather, or slice into more manageable squares. Use as needed.

6. To store: place in food-grade bag. Take away as much air from the bag before sealing. Store at room temperature or in the fridge. Vegetable leather should be consumed within three days for maximum flavor.

Dehydrating:

Additional equipment: food grade bags, offset spatula, saran wrap

1. Preheat machine to highest setting.

2. Line trays with saran wrap with small overhangs on each. This makes it easier to peel off vegetable leather later on.

3. Pour small amount of processed vegetables on the trays. Spread to about ⅛-inch thick using an offset spatula.

4. Dehydrate for four to six hours. Rotate trays every hour. Vegetable leather is done when this is no longer tacky, but still pliable.

5. Turn off heat. Cool completely to room temperature. Remove vegetable leather from trays.

6. Either leave whole, or slice into squares. Use as needed.

7. To store: place in food-grade bag. Take away as much air from the bag before sealing. Store at room temperature, or in the fridge. Vegetable leather should be consumed within three days for maximum flavor.

Chapter 6: Herbs and Spices

Drying Herbs and Spices

Most herbs and spices are easy to grow at home, and many can be grown in small containers on your balcony, porch or any area of your house or yard that gets regular sunlight. In addition to being a considerable way to flavor foods, herbs and spices have a number of health benefits associated with them.

Drying is the convenient way to preserve herbs and spices because all you usually have to do is lay out the leaves, flowers or seeds and let them dry and then grind or crush them as you see fit. Herbs and spices should be dried in a dehydrator because drying them in the sun can bring them to lose some of their potency.

The following herbs and spices are good candidates for drying:

- Bay.
- Celery leaves.
- Chervil.
- Chicory.
- Chives.

- Cilantro.

- Cinnamon sticks.

- Cloves.

- Dill.

- Laurel.

- Marjoram.

- Mint.

- Oregano.

- Parsley.

- Peppercorns.

- Rosemary.

- Sage.

- Summer savory.

- Tarragon.

- Thyme.

Harvest herbs and spices by removing them from the plant in the early morning. Harvest them before the flowers open and be careful not to damage them during the harvest. Do not attempt to dry damaged pieces. The drying process isn't going to make damaged herbs and spices any better.

Lay the herbs or spices out in a single layer on the dehydrator tray and spread them out so there's a bit of space between them for air circulation. Most herbs and spices should be dried at temperatures between 115 and 125 degrees F, but be assured to check the documentation that came with your dehydrator to see what the recommended temperature for drying herbs and spices is.

The drying time for herbs and spices should be short. Most herbs and spices should be done drying in less than 4 hours. Herbs and spices are done when they feel crispy and are brittle to the touch. You should be able to crumble leaves, stems and flowers between your fingers.

Some herbs and spices can be hung out to air dry. Rosemary, thyme, sage and parsley can all be hung inside the house and left to dry. Basil, oregano and mint leaves need to be placed inside a paper bag before being hung out to dry. Air-drying can be done indoors or out, but be sure to hang the herbs and spices in a shaded area if drying them outside. Air-drying herbs by hanging them can take a week or two to properly dry the herbs. Herbs and some spices can be dried in the microwave if you're in a hurry. Microwave them on high for 2 minutes and check them. If they're still wet, microwave them for 30 seconds and check them again. Continue microwaving the herbs in 30-second increments until they're done drying.

Storing Herbs and Spices

Here's the dilemma. Herbs and spices will last a lot longer when they're left whole, but they're usually ground or crushed when they're used in recipes. It's kind of a hassle to grind or crush your herbs every time you want to use them, especially when you're looking to make a quick meal. What I do is dry a large batch of herbs and spices. I crush up half of it and store it that way, so I always have crushed or ground herbs and spices on hand. I then store the rest of it in the freezer whole. When I start to run low, I crush or grind the herbs I have in the freezer and I'm ready to go. I know when I pull a batch out of the freezer, I'm going to need to dry more soon or I'm going to run out.

Chapter 7: Meat and Poultry

Making Jerky

- Beef, pork, venison, wild game and smoked turkey breast can be dry preserved to produce a dried meat product that is protein rich, does not need refrigeration, is easily stored and lightweight to carry. Best results are obtained from lean meat sources.

- Health Concerns

- Trichinellosis/Trichinosis

- This is a disease caused by the consumption of undercooked or raw meat from animals infected with a microscopic parasite known as Trichinella.

- The infection occurs most commonly in wild, meat eating animals such as wild boar. For in depth information related to all aspects of this infection you can source plenty of reputable information from the Centers for Disease Control And

Prevention   at

www.cdc.gov/parasites/trichinellosis/gen_info/faqs.html.

- If you are planning to use wild game or pork to make jerky you need to treat the meat first in order to kill the trichinella parasite prior to slicing and marinating.

- Treating Meat to Kill the Trichinella Parasite

- Your meat should be cut into strips not exceeding 6 inches thick. You should then freeze these strips at 0°F or less for at least 30 days.

Safe Handling Of Meat And Poultry

- All raw meats can become contaminated with microorganisms that cause disease. Use the process outlined below as the most basic guide to the safe handling of poultry and meat.

- Rinse hands thoroughly with soap and running water both prior to and after handling raw meat.

- Ensure that all utensils and equipment have been properly cleaned.

- Clean your utensils and equipment prior to preparing different meat sources.

- Poultry and meat should be refrigerated at temperatures less than 40°F. Red meat should be used within 5 days. If not used within 5 days it has to be frozen. Ground beef or poultry should be used within 2 days. If not used within 2 days it has to be frozen

- Frozen meat should never be let thaw on a countertop/worktable etc. Frozen meat should always be thawed out in a refrigerator.

- Meat should always be left to marinate in a refrigerator. Never leave meat to marinate outside the refrigerator.

- Never re-use marinade or save it for future use.

Making Jerky from Wild Game

There are several extra factors to consider when making jerky from wild game.

Be aware of the possibility of Trichinellosis as described earlier.

Be aware of the possibility of fecal bacteria which can contaminate the meat. This often occurs as a result of animal gut contents coming into contact with the meat because of the location of the wound. It can also happen as an emanate of the transfer of bacteria from the hunter's hands which might have been in contact with the animals gut content.

Meat that has been contaminated in this manner should never be used for making jerky. If it is to be used for other purposes it should be only used in ways which require thorough cooking through of the meat.

Deer Jerky: to lessen the chances of bacterial growth deer carcasses should always be rapidly chilled.

Preparing Your Meat

- Make slicing easier by partially freezing your meat.

- Ideally, your meat slices should not exceed ¼ inch.

- Remove as much fat as possible.

- If you prefer chewy jerky slice your meat with the grain.

- If you prefer brittle jerky, slice your meat across the grain.

- If desired, you can also use a tenderizer to break up the meat fibers.

- Marinades can be used to add flavor and increase tenderness.
- Marinade recipes will include common ingredients such as salt, spices and oils as well as acidic ingredients such as lemon juice, vinegar, teriyaki and soy sauce.

How to Prepare a Jerky Marinade

You will need

- Approximately 2 lbs of your preferred meat.
- 1 teaspoon of hickory flavor salt.
- ¼ teaspoon of black pepper.
- ¼ teaspoon of onion powder.
- 1 tablespoon of Worcestershire sauce.
- ¼ cup soy sauce.

Method

1. Add all of your ingredients in a bowl and mix.
2. Using uniform sized strips of meat, no more than ¼ inch thick place them in a pan.
3. Now cover the meat strips with the ingredients from the bowl.
4. Cover your pan.
5. Refrigerate for 2 to 3 hours. If you prefer a salty taste you can leave your strips marinating for longer.

As discussed earlier there is a method for decreasing the chances of foodborne illness. If you want to do this, now is the time to do it. Simply do the following.

1. directly after your desired marinating time, bring your meat strips in the marinade to a boil and continue to boil for a

further 5 minutes. If your meat strips are larger than the recommended ¼ inch thick you should boil for 10 minutes.

2. when the boiling time has elapsed you should remove your strips, drain and dry.

3. The ideal temperature you are seeking for is 160°F in the middle of the meat strips. This is a more accurate and safe method than using general time limits as it allows for variances in the thickness of strips. To be absolutely sure, use a thermometer and keep all your meat strips at the same size.

How to Dry Your Meat If Using A Marinade

- Drain off and dispose of marinade.
- Remove strips of meat and place on clean dry absorbent towels.
- Use dehydrator trays or cake racks placed on baking sheets, if you plan to oven dry your meat.
- Leave a small gap between each slice to allow for even distribution of hot air. Do not have meat strips overlapping or touching.
- Have your oven or dehydrator pre-heated to 140°F.
- It is best to utilize a test piece first. This will take about 3 hours. Your test strips of meat should crack and bend but not break.
- Heated marinated meats will dry a lot faster than meat that has not been heated in marinade. Heated marinated meat will take 3 – 4 hours depending on size. Non-heated marinated meat will take between 10 to 24 hours.

- Use the doneness test described in number 6, when meat is dried remove it from the oven and pat dry using clean, dry absorbent towels. Leave strips on rack to cool a little.

- When strips have cooled enough to handle easily, remove from rack and let them cool down totally.

- When your meat strips have totally cooled, place them in heavy, food grade, plastic storage bags. If desired you can also vacuum pack your meat.

Foodborne Illness

I described the method earlier for reducing foodborne illness risks by boiling your meat strips in the marinade directly after removing them from the refrigerator. If you did not use that option you can now use the option described below.

- Place your dried meat slices on a baking sheet.

- Leave a little space between them, do not have your meat touching or overlapping.

- Place the meat in a pre-heated oven of 275°F for 10 minutes. If your slices are thicker than the recommended ¼ inch thickness you will need to leave them inside the oven until it reaches the internal temperature of the strips reaches 160°F. Use a metal stem thermometer to test.

How to Make Jerky From Ground Meat

- It is more difficult to reduce the risk of bacterial infection with ground meat than it is with whole meat pieces.

- Great care is necessary to be taken when handling the meat.

- Always follow the procedures as described in the section on Safe Handling Of Meat And Poultry.

- Always follow the directions provided by the dehydrator manufacturer.

- Use different presses for shaping your meat but always thoroughly clean those shapers before switching meat types.

- The key to food safety during the entire jerky making process is to follow all safety procedures and always ensure that the internal temperature of your meat reaches 160°F. A metal stem thermometer is your best friend in this process.

How to Store Your Jerky

- To maintain both the flavor and quality of your jerky it is always best to refrigerate or freeze it. If you are not refrigerating or freezing your jerky will only last for two weeks in a sealed container at room temperature.

Chapter 8: Seafood

- Salmon Jerky

Preparation time: 30 minutes

Cooking time/Dry: 8 hours

Servings: 4

INGREDIENTS:

- 1 1/4 pounds skin-on salmon
- 1/2 cup soy sauce
- 1 tablespoon light brown sugar
- 1 tablespoon fresh lime juice
- 1 teaspoon black pepper
- 1 pinch dried hot chili powder

DIRECTIONS:

1. Place salmon, skin side down, on a clean work surface. Run your hand against the grain of the fish, feeling for bones. Using tweezers or fish pliers, remove all bones.

2. Transfer salmon to a zipper bag (or wrap in plastic wrap) and freeze for 1 hour. This makes it easier for you to cut.

3. While salmon freezes, mix remaining ingredients in a medium bowl.

4. Remove salmon from freezer and slice with the grain into long, narrow strips. Each strip should be 1/4" thick by 1"–2" wide by 3"–4" long.

5. Toss salmon into the marinade and cover the bowl. Marinate in your refrigerator for 11/2–3 hours.

6. Line three dehydrator racks completely with plastic wrap. Brush with vegetable oil or spray with pan spray. Remove each salmon strip from marinade using tongs. Shake over bowl to remove excess marinade and place in a single layer on rack. Repeat with remaining salmon strips.

7. Place racks into dehydrator and set to 145°F.

8. Check salmon after 3 hours. Jerky is ready when it's dry to the touch, and snaps when bent. If jerky is not dry, check again in an hour. Depending on the thickness of your strips, the circulation of your dehydrator, and the amount of marinade you were able to remove from the jerky, it may take up to 8 hours to dry.

9. Once jerky is dry, remove rack from dehydrator and allow jerky to cool to room temperature, about 2 hours. Transfer to an airtight container and store.

NUTRITION: Calories: 866 Protein: 133.24 g Fat: 33.93 g. Carbs: 7.16 g

48. Scallops

Preparation time: 30 minutes

Cooking time/Dry: 10 hours

Servings: 4

INGREDIENTS:

- 1 pound raw scallops, each scallop's "foot" removed
- 1 roll paper towels
- 1 teaspoon salt

DIRECTIONS:

1. Split each scallop in half lengthwise. Pat scallop halves dry with paper towel and sprinkle evenly with salt.
2. Spread scallops in a single even layer, cut side up, across one or more dehydrator shelves. Dehydrate at 145°F until dry to the touch and very firm, about 8–10 hours.
3. Transfer scallops to a clean work surface and cool to room temperature, about 2 hours. Transfer to an airtight container and store.
4. Uses
5. Rehydrate scallops with steam or simmering water for 1–2 hours. Drain, pat dry, and roughly chop.
6. Use rehydrated conpoy in a mixed seafood salad with other shellfish such as shrimp and squid. Make a tangy lime dressing with just a touch of hot sauce.
7. Add dried scallops to sautéed green vegetables, such as broccoli or bok choy.

NUTRITION: Calories: 98 Protein: 14.65 g Fat: 1.02 g.Carbs: 6.65 g

49. Shrimp

Preparation time: 30 minutes

Cooking time: 3 minutes

Servings: 4

INGREDIENTS:

- 1 tablespoon salt
- 1 pound raw shrimp, peeled, deveined, and tails removed

DIRECTIONS:

1. Bring a large pot of water to a rolling boil. Add salt and bring back to a boil. Add shrimp and cook, uncovered, until shrimp is bright pink, about 3 minutes.

2. Drain shrimp and plunge into ice water to chill. Drain and blot with paper towels.

3. Split each shrimp in half lengthwise.

4. Spread shrimp in a single even layer, cut side up, across one or more dehydrator shelves. Dehydrate at 145°F until dry to the touch and very firm, about 3–5 hours.

5. Transfer shrimp to a clean work surface and cool to room temperature, about 2 hours. Transfer to an airtight container and store.

6. Uses

7. Dried shrimp make a great addition to your favorite fried rice recipe. Rehydrate shrimp, drain, and chop finely. Then add as the final ingredient before serving.

8. Make homemade Cantonese XO sauce with dried shrimp. Combine 1/2 cup dried shrimp, 1/4 cup dried hot chili peppers, 1 tablespoon dried garlic, and 1 cup vegetable oil (such as canola oil or safflower oil) in a blender. Purée until smooth. Use as a condiment to add spice, salt, and umami to stir-fried dishes.

9. You can pulverize dried shrimp using a food processor. Once you powder shrimp, use it to boost the flavor of seafood gumbo or shrimp bisque, or as a condiment that adds both a salty and shrimplike flavor.

10. That Annoying Fish Smell

11. Some foods while they're dehydrating spread wonderful smells around your house, but some don't. Fish fits into that latter category. If you don't want your house smelling like you has been cooking fish for weeks on end, crank open a window before you start dehydrating.

12. Herbs and Dairy

13. One of the bright spots in any garden is a section of herbs growing in a sunny patch. With a quick trip out to this part of your garden, you can add freshness and flavor to any dish. As most gardeners know, it's challenging to use all your fresh herbs before the growing season is done. Enter drying! Your own dehydrated herbs pack much more flavor than the store-bought herbs—plus you never feel like you've got to let your garden's bounty go to waste.

14. What applies to herbs also applies to dairy. So often, you'll have a drawer full of half-eaten cheeses. By dehydrating and then pulverizing cheese, you get cheese powder, which lasts much

longer than cheese, and is a great staple for sprinkling on snack foods or adding to soups and stews.

NUTRITION: Calories: 113 Protein: 23.16 g Fat: 1.54 g. Carbs: 0 g

Chapter 9: Breads, Crackers, and Chips

50. Vegan Bread

Preparation time: 30 minutes

Cooking time: 6 hours

Servings: 6

INGREDIENTS:

- 1 head cauliflower
- 1 teaspoon turmeric
- 2 tablespoons flax seed
- 1/2 cup psyllium hust
- 1/2 cup brewer's yeast
- 4 large zucchini
- Salt and black pepper

DIRECTIONS:

1. Place cauliflower and zucchini in a food processor and pulse until they form a paste. Add the turmeric, flax seeds, psyllium, yeast, and a pinch of salt and black pepper. Pulse again until all ingredients are thoroughly combined.

2. Place ParaFlexx Screens on the racks of your Excalibur Food Dehydrator. Form the mixture into slices about 1/2-inch-thick, and place on the screens.

3. Set your Excalibur to 150F and dehydrate for 6 hours. The bread should not be completely dry. One side should be slightly soft.

NUTRITION: Calories: 219 Fat: 1.9 g, Carbs: 61.6 g Protein: 10.1 g.

51. Fluffy Dinner Rolls

Preparation time: 15 minutes

Cooking time: 7 hours

Servings: 6

INGREDIENTS:

- 2 cups almond flour

- 1 cup psyllium

- 3 tablespoons ground flax seeds

- 1 tablespoon onion powder

- 2 teaspoons garlic powder

- 1 tablespoon lemon juice

- 1 teaspoon salt

- 1/3 cup water

DIRECTIONS:

1. In a large bowl, combine the flour, psyllium, flax seeds, onion powder, garlic powder, lemon juice, salt, and water. Mix well until combined.

2. Form the mixture into 6 round rolls.

3. Place ParaFlexx Screens on the racks of your Excalibur. Place the rolls on the screens so they are not touching. Dehydrate at 145F for one hour, and then lower the temperature to 110F for the remaining 6 hours. Remove from the screens and serve warm or allow cooling before storing.

NUTRITION: Calories: 319 Fat: 7.1 g,Carbs: 95.2 g Protein: 3.5 g.

52. Herb and Almond Crackers

Preparation time: 10 minutes

Cooking time: 12 hours

Servings: 6

INGREDIENTS:

- 2 cups almonds
- 1/2 cup ground flax seeds
- 1/4 cup brewer's yeast
- 3/4 cups water
- 2 tablespoons fresh rosemary, finely chopped
- 1 teaspoon salt
- 1/2 teaspoon black pepper

DIRECTIONS:

1. In a food processor, combine the almonds, flax seed, yeast, salt, and pepper. Pulse until well combined.

2. Slowly add the water while continuing to pulse until a paste forms.

3. Place ParaFlexx Screens on the racks of your Excalibur and spread a thin layer of the paste onto each screen. Set your Excalibur to 115F and dehydrate for 12 hours or until the crackers are crispy. Remove from the screens and break into small pieces to serve.

NUTRITION: Calories: 260 Fat: 19.3 g, Carbs: 13.3 g Protein: 11.6 g.

53. Carrot Crackers

Preparation time: 20 minutes

Cooking time: 12 hours

Servings: 12

INGREDIENTS:

- 6 large carrots, peeled
- 1/2 cup ground flax seeds
- 1 tomato, diced
- Juice from 1 lemon
- 1/2 cup sesame seeds
- 1/2 cup chia seeds
- 3/4 cups water

DIRECTIONS:

1. In a food processor, combine the carrots, flax seeds, tomato, lemon juice, and water, and pulse until a paste forms. Add the chia seeds and sesame seeds and stir to combine.

2. Place ParaFlexx Screens on the racks of your Excalibur Food Dehydrator. Spread the paste evenly on the screens about 1/4 inch thick.

3. Set your Excalibur to 105F and dehydrate for 12 hours. Remove the crackers from the Excalibur and allow cooling completely. The crackers will become crispy as they cool.

NUTRITION: Calories: 122 Fat: 7.4 g, Carbs: 10.8 g Protein: 3.9 g.

54. Sweet Potato Chips

Preparation time: 10 minutes

Cooking time: 12 to 14 hours

Servings: 6

INGREDIENTS:

- 2 large sweet potatoes
- 2 teaspoons coconut oil, melted
- 2 teaspoons salt

DIRECTIONS:

1. Using a mandolin, slice the potatoes into thin rounds. In a large bowl, combine the potato slices, salt, and coconut oil and toss to coat.
2. Place ParaFlexx Screens on the racks of your Excalibur Food Dehydrator and place the potato slices on the screens in a single layer.
3. Set your Excalibur to 125F and dehydrate for 12 to 14 hours or until the potato slices are crisp. Remove from the screens and store in a cool dry place if not using immediately.

NUTRITION: Calories: 13 Fat: 1.5 g Carbs: 0.1 g Protein: 0 g.

Chapter 10: Breakfast

55. Tasty Pineapple Chunks

Preparation Time: 10 minutes

Cooking time: 12 hours

Serving: 4

INGREDIENT:

- 1 ripe pineapple

DIRECTIONS:

1. Peel and cut pineapple. Cut in half and then cut each half in ¼ inch thick chunks.

2. Place pineapple chunks on dehydrator racks and dehydrate at 135 F/ 58 C for 12 hours.

NUTRITION: Calories: 62 Total Fat: 0.2g Protein: 0.7g Carbs: 16.2g

56. Dried Mango

Preparation Time: 5 Minutes

Cooking Time: 8 Hours

Serving: 2

INGREDIENTS:

- ½ mango, peeled, pitted, and cut into ⅜-inch slices

DIRECTIONS:

1. Arrange the mango slices flat in a single layer in the Cook & Crisp Basket. Place in the pot and close the Crisping Lid.
2. Press Dehydrate, set the temperature to 135°F, and set the time to 8 hours. Select Start/Stop to begin.
3. When dehydrating is complete, remove the basket from the pot and transfer the mango slices to an airtight container.

NUTRITION: Calories: 67 Fiber: 2g. Protein: 1g Carbohydrates: 18g.

57. Beet Chips

Preparation Time: 5 Minutes

Cooking Time: 8 Hours

Serving: ½ Cup

INGREDIENTS:

- ½ beet, peeled and cut into ⅛-inch slices

DIRECTIONS:

1. Arrange the beet slices flat in a single layer in the Cook & Crisp Basket. Place in the pot and close the Crisping Lid.
2. Press Dehydrate, set the temperature to 135°F, and set the time to 8 hours. Select Start/Stop to begin.
3. When dehydrating is complete, remove the basket from the pot and transfer the beet chips to an airtight container.

TIP: Use a mandolin to ensure that the beet is sliced evenly into consistent ⅛-inch slices.

NUTRITION: Calories: 35 Sodium: 64mg Carbohydrates: 8g Fiber: 2g Protein: 1g

58. Loaded Smashed Potatoes

Preparation Time: 10 Minutes

Cooking Time: 30 Minutes

Serving: 4

INGREDIENTS:

- 12 ounces baby Yukon Gold potatoes
- 1 teaspoon extra-virgin olive oil
- ¼ cup sour cream
- ¼ cup shredded Cheddar cheese
- 2 slices bacon, cooked and crumbled
- 1 tablespoon chopped fresh chives
- Sea salt

DIRECTIONS:

1. Place the Cook & Crisp Basket in the pot. Close the Crisping Lid. Preheat the unit by selecting Air Crisp, setting the temperature to 350°F, and setting the time to 5 minutes. Press Start/Stop to begin.

2. Meanwhile, toss the potatoes with the oil until evenly coated.

3. Once the pot and basket are preheated, open the lid and add the potatoes to the basket. Close the lid, select Air Crisp, set the temperature to 350°F, and set the time to 30 minutes. Press Start/Stop to begin.

4. After 15 minutes, open the lid, then lift the basket and shake the potatoes. Lower the basket back into the pot and close the lid to resume cooking.

5. After 15 minutes, check the potatoes for your desired crispiness. They should be fork tender.

6. Remove the potatoes from the basket. Use a large spoon to lightly crush the potatoes to split them. Top with the sour cream, cheese, bacon, and chives, and season with salt.

NUTRITION: Calories: 154 Fat: 8g Carbohydrates: 16g Protein: 5g

59. Fruity Guacamole

Preparation Time: 10 minutes

Cooking Time: 0

Serving: 8

INGREDIENTS:

- 2 large avocados, peeled and pitted
- 1 cup of mango, peeled, pitted and cubed
- ½ small red onion, chopped
- ¼ cup of fresh cilantro, chopped
- 1 cup of fresh strawberries, hulled and chopped
- 1 tablespoon of fresh lime juice

DIRECTIONS:

1. In a large serving bowl, place the avocado flesh and mash roughly. Add the remaining ingredients and gently, stir to combine. Serve immediately.

NUTRITION: Calories: 107 Protein: 1.2g Carbs: 8.6g Fat: 8.4g

60. Strawberry Gazpacho

Preparation Time: 10 minutes

Cooking Time: 0

Serving: 6

INGREDIENTS:

- 2 pounds of fresh strawberries, hulled
- ½ cup of red bell pepper, seeded and chopped
- ½ cup of fresh basil leaves
- ¼ cup of organic apple cider vinegar
- 1 small cumber, peeled, seeded and chopped
- ½ cup of onion, chopped
- 1 small garlic clove, peeled
- 1 tablespoon of extra-virgin olive oil

DIRECTIONS:

1. In a blender, add all the ingredients and pulse until smooth. Transfer the gazpacho into a large bowl. Cover and refrigerate to chill before serving.

NUTRITION: Calories: 86 Protein: 1.7g Carbs: 15.4g Fat: 2.9g

61. Strawberry Smoothie Bowl

Preparation Time: 10 minutes

Cooking Time: 0

Serving: 2

INGREDIENTS:

- 2¼ cups of frozen strawberries
- ¼ cup low-fat plain Greek yogurt
- 2 tablespoons of almonds, chopped
- ½ cup of unsweetened almond milk
- ¼ cup fresh strawberries, hulled and sliced

DIRECTIONS:

1. In a blender, add frozen strawberries and pulse for about 1 minute. Add the almond milk and yogurt and pulse until desired consistency is achieved. Transfer the mixture into 2 serving bowls evenly. Serve immediately with the topping of strawberry slices and almonds.

NUTRITION: Calories: 124 Protein: 4.5g Carbs: 17.8g Fat: 4.8g

62. Mango Smoothie Bowl

Preparation Time: 10 minutes

Cooking Time: 0

Serving: 2

INGREDIENTS:

- 1½ cups of frozen mango chunks
- 1 teaspoon of organic apple cider vinegar
- ½ teaspoon of ground turmeric
- 1 tablespoon of raw honey
- 1 tablespoon unsweetened coconut, shredded
- ½ cup cooked sweet potato, chopped
- 1 tablespoon of chia seeds
- ¼ teaspoon of ground cinnamon
- 1 cup unsweetened almond milk

DIRECTIONS:

1. In a blender, add all the ingredients except for coconut and pulse until desired consistency is achieved. Transfer the mixture into 2 serving bowls evenly. Serve immediately with the topping of coconut.

NUTRITION: Calories: 108 Protein: 3.4g Carbs: 41g Fat: 4.5g

63. Berries Yogurt Bowl

Preparation Time: 10 minutes

Cooking Time: 0

Serving: 2

INGREDIENTS:

- 1½ cups of low-fat plain Greek Yogurt
- ½ cup of fresh strawberries, hulled and sliced
- 2 tablespoons of almonds, chopped
- ½ cup of fresh blueberries
- 1 tablespoon of raw honey

DIRECTIONS:

1. In a large bowl, add top with berries, followed by honey and almonds. Serve immediately.

NUTRITION: Calories: 229 Protein: 12.3g Carbs: 30.9g Fat: 5.5g

64. Apple Yogurt Bowl

Preparation Time: 10 minutes

Cooking Time: 0

Serving: 2

INGREDIENTS:

- 1¼ cups of low-fat plain Greek Yogurt
- ¼ teaspoon of ground cinnamon
- 2 tablespoons of almonds, chopped
- 2 teaspoons of extra-virgin olive oil
- 2 large apples, cored and cubed

DIRECTIONS:

1. In a large bowl, add the yogurt, oil and cinnamon and mix until well combined. Gently, fold in the apple cubes. Divide the yogurt mixture in 2 serving bowls. Top with almonds and serve immediately.

NUTRITION: Calories: 300 Protein: 10.6g Carbs: 43.1g Fat: 9.9g

65. Dehydrated Blueberry Vegetable Pancakes

Preparation Time: 30 minutes

Cooking/Dry Time: 13 hours

Serving: 2

INGREDIENTS:

- 200 ml soy milk
- 90 g bise flour
- 15 g neutral oil (rapeseed, sunflower, etc.)
- 10 g starch (epifine, potato or corn)
- 2 tablespoons dehydrated blueberries
- 1/2 tsp. baking powder
- 1/2 tsp. apple vinegar
- 1 sachet of vanilla sugar (about 10 g)
- 1 pinch of salt

DIRECTIONS:

1. How to dry blueberries
2. Fill up with blueberries in its peak season (between July and September). To dehydrate blueberries, we recommend using a dehydrator such as Excalibur or Sedona.
3. Prepare your blueberries by washing them and then place them on your trays over the entire surface. Do not hesitate to tighten them because their volume will reduce during drying.
4. Turn on your dehydrator, depending on the temperature; dehydration will take between 8 and 13 hours.

5. The advantage of doing it yourself is that you will hardly find dried blueberries commercially. So fill your jars, you will have a thousand and one opportunities to enjoy yourself by incorporating these dried fruits in yogurt, muesli, muffins, cakes, etc.

6. How to make vegetable pancakes with dehydrated blueberries

7. In a bowl, and then mix the dry ingredients (except blueberries). Make a well and add the vinegar and oil. Start mixing gently with a whisk and add the soy milk. Whisk until you get a smooth paste.

8. In a small oiled pan heated over high heat (but not to the maximum), pour the dough using a small ladle. Let cook until the dough is "dry" on top and turn over for about thirty seconds (you just need to brown the other side a little).

9. Serve hot with maple syrup and a few more dehydrated blueberries.

NUTRITION: Calories: 311 Protein: 8.58 g Fat: 8.1 g Carbs: 51.89 g

Chapter 11: Main Meals

66. Mushroom Velouté

Preparation Time: 30 minutes

Cooking/Dry Time: 13 hours

Serving: 2

INGREDIENTS:

- 1 large egg
- 200ml fresh milk
- 1 tablespoon mushroom mixture
- 1 tablespoon grated cheese
- For the mushroom mixture:
- 1.7 oz. dried mushrooms
- A sprig of dried parsley
- 1/8 cup potato flour

DIRECTIONS:

1. For the mixture, blend the mushrooms and dried parsley until you get a fine-grained mixture such as flour. Add the starch and operate the mixer to mix well, and then pour the mixture into a jar. For the Velouté, dilute the mushroom preparation with a little milk in a saucepan then slowly, always stirring, the rest of the milk, put the saucepan on the heat over a gentle flame, season with salt and turn occasionally to prevent the cream from sticking. When it starts to thicken, remove from the heat, and add the grated cheese and the butter nut, mix and serve.

NUTRITION: Calories: 255 Protein: 9.03 g Fat: 7.46 g Carbs: 34.05 g

67. Cherry Chicken Salad

Preparation Time: 30 minutes

Cooking Time: 30 minutes

Serving: 2

INGREDIENTS:

- 400g/2.86 cups boneless chicken, diced
- ½ cup rehydrated cherries (or dried if you like the intense taste)
- Chopped leek
- Celery in small pieces
- Fresh mint chopped pleasure
- 5/6 lettuce leaves
- For the vinaigrette
- 125ml Extra Virgin Olive Oil
- 2 tbsp. raspberry syrup
- 1 tbsp. Dijon mustard
- Salt
- Pepper

DIRECTIONS:

1. Combine the chicken cubes previously cooked in a pan, the cherries, leek, mustard and mint in a salad bowl.
2. For the vinaigrette mix the Ingredients then pour it into the salad bowl and stir.
3. Serve on a bed of lettuce leaves.

NUTRITION: Calories: 341 Protein: 31.37 g Fat: 19.8 g Carbs: 8.1 g

68. Vegetable Omelette

Preparation Time: 30 minutes

Cooking Time: 15 minutes

Serving: 4

INGREDIENTS:

- 6 eggs
- 6 tablespoons of vegetables and dried herbs and spices to taste (zucchini, peppers, eggplants, cherry tomatoes, oregano, basil, onion, chili, mushrooms etc.)
- 6 tablespoons milk
- Salt and pepper
- Grated parmesan to taste
- Oil or butter

DIRECTIONS:

1. Put the dried vegetables and herbs and spices in a little warm water for about 20 minutes; if necessary, reduce them into small pieces before soaking them. Meanwhile prepare the omelet: beat the eggs in a bowl with milk, season with pepper and salt. Drain and gently squeeze the vegetables, sauté them in a pan for about 15 minutes. Some products with mushrooms may take a little longer, so check the cooking time before proceeding. Pour the eggs into the pan and cook like a normal omelet, turning every once a while.

NUTRITION: Calories: 297 Protein: 22.66 g Fat: 16.46 g Carbs: 13.65 g

69. Mushroom Meatballs and Chard Leaf Curry

Preparation Time: 30 minutes

Cooking/Dry Time: 8 hours

Serving: 4

INGREDIENTS:

- 6 champignon mushrooms
- 1/2 cup sesame seeds
- 1/2 cup pumpkin seeds
- Curry
- Chard leaves
- Salt
- Herbs
- Garlic
- Shallots
- Parsley

DIRECTIONS:

1. Blend all the Ingredients until you get a homogeneous dough then form meatballs and dry at 104- 113 degrees for about 8 hours. Wrap each meatball in a chard leaf and serve.

2. If you want requires the dish prepared an avocado mayonnaise. The latter is obtained by blending the avocado with Evo oil salt and lemon juice

NUTRITION: Calories: 210 Protein: 9.14 g Fat: 18.84 g Carbs: 5.54 g

70. Cous Cous Meatballs with Melissa and Green Beans

Preparation Time: 30 minutes

Cooking Time: 15 minutes

Serving: 4

INGREDIENTS:

- 320ml water
- 1 cup pre-cooked couscous
- 2 tbsp. dried herbs to taste
- Green beans
- Melissa
- 1 egg
- Breadcrumbs
- Salt
- 4-5 walnuts
- Extra Virgin Olive Oil

DIRECTIONS:

1. Bring the water to a boil with a pinch of salt and dried herbs, then remove from the heat and leave covered for a couple of minutes to flavor well. Filter and pour the broth on the couscous, diluting well until the liquid is fully absorbed. Meanwhile, boil the green beans for 20 minutes in the pressure cooker, then let them cool and cut into rounds of about zero 0.5 cm. In a bowl mix the egg, breadcrumbs, couscous, a nice eat? Dried lemon balm flowers and the nuts previously pulverized in the mixer,

then season with the breadcrumbs and oil. Or if necessary, add salt

2. Make meatballs with your hands and place them on the baking tray covered with parchment paper. Before baking at 356 degrees for about 15 minutes cover the surface of the meatballs with a drizzle of oil.

NUTRITION: Calories: 293 Protein: 8.63 g Fat: 23.39 g Carbs: 15.59 g

71. Falafel

Preparation Time: 30 minutes

Cooking/Dry Time: 3 hours

Serving: 4

INGREDIENTS:

- 2 champignon mushrooms
- 2 carrots
- 1/2 onion
- 1 garlic clove
- 3 tbsp. oil
- Salt pepper
- Cumin, parsley, paprika, coriander
- Juice of 1 lemon
- 3.5oz pistachios /3.5oz walnuts /3.5oz sunflower seeds
- 3 dried tomatoes rehydrated
- Sesame seeds

DIRECTIONS:

1. Chop carrots, onion, tomatoes, mushrooms and garlic then season with salt oil. Blend coarsely pistachios, walnuts and sunflower seeds, add them to vegetables and season with spices and lemon juice.

2. Season with salt, make meatballs and roll them into sesame seeds. Finally, dry at 104 degrees for 2 or 3 hours and consume immediately.

NUTRITION: Calories: 278 Protein: 7.15 g Fat: 23.46 g Carbs: 14.34 g

Chapter 12: Desserts

72. Mega Chocolate Cake in a Dehydrator Rawmid Dream Vitamin Ddv-07

Preparation Time: 30 minutes

Cooking Time: 2 hours

Serving: 4

INGREDIENTS:

- KORZHI:
- 60 g of walnuts - pre-washed and soaked for several hours
- 160 ml Jerusalem artichoke syrup or any other vegetable syrup
- 70 g ripe sweet apple
- 1/4 Art (50-80 ml) strong boiled coffee (I used espresso)
- 1 tbsp. l martini (can be replaced with another preferred drink)
- 1/2 tsp. vanilla sugar
- 1-2 tsp. lemon juice
- 1/8 tsp. salt
- 50 g cocoa powder
- 115 g coconut flour
- Chocolate Cream:
- 260-300 g avocado pulp
- 160 ml Jerusalem artichoke syrup or any other vegetable syrup
- 2 tbsp. l Martini
- 1/2 tsp. vanilla sugar
- 1 tbsp. l lemon juice
- 1/8 tsp. salt
- 50 g cocoa powder

- For additional decoration, you can use chocolate chips, cocoa nibs or pieces of chocolate.

DIRECTIONS:

1. We make cakes

2. In a blender, beat in a uniform mass washed and pre-soaked walnuts, syrup, apple, coffee, martini, vanilla sugar, lemon juice and salt.

3. Carefully pour coconut flour into a blender

4. And process on a pulsed basis until the mixture becomes like a slightly crumbly dough.

5. We return to the cake.

6. Divide the resulting dough into 2 equal parts.

7. Spread the first half in a small mold. For these purposes, I used a form for making tofu, having previously laid it with a sheet of cellophane. The dough needs to be thoroughly crushed and tamped.

8. By the way, the tofu mold for this stage fits perfectly: with the help of a "lid" that fits inside the mold, easily compacts the laid out mass.

9. On a metal baking sheet of a RawMid Dream Vitamin DDV-07 dehydrator, put a plastic wire sheet. We carefully remove the thick cake from the mold and immediately place it on the prepared baking sheet of the dehydrator. We repeat the procedure with the second piece of dough - we ram the cake and put it on a baking sheet, next to the first.

10. Turn on the dehydrator RawMid Dream Vitamin DDV-07. We set the temperature in the menu from 60 to 70 ° C, as well as the cooking time - 2 hours. Close the shutter. The process has begun!

11. Cakes are ready, as soon as their surface is noticeably dry, it will become hard and somewhat rough.

12. Whip cream

13. An important point: for chocolate cream, choose the ripest, soft avocados - then the taste will be rich.

14. We put all the products necessary for the cream in a blender. Pour cocoa powder last!

15. Beat products until smooth cream. Everything is almost ready with us!

16. Making a cake

17. Remove from the pan our cakes. We put one cake on a dish; evenly and generously cover its surface with chocolate cream.

18. We place the second cake on top - we also cover it with cream, leaving a high "cap" at the top. Coat the sides of the cake with cream.

19. Using a teaspoon, we form sharp and beautiful "peaks" on the cream.

20. We put the cake in the refrigerator overnight.

21. Before serving, sprinkle the surface of the cake with chocolate chips or cocoa. The cake is very conveniently cut; the cream does not lose shape.

22. Store dessert in a refrigerator in a closed container for up to 4 days.

NUTRITION: Calories: 306 Protein: 7.55 g Fat: 16.73 g Carbs: 35.61 g

73. Piquant of Roasted Cashews

Preparation Time: 30 minutes

Cooking Time: 16-20 hours

Serving: 4

INGREDIENTS:

- 220 g fried cashews
- 180 ml of liquid from sauerkraut (possible with slices of sauerkraut)
- 2 tbsp. l coconut oil
- 3 large pinches of Dulce algae
- 3-4 tbsp. l lemon juice
- 1-1.5 tsp. spices based on red bell pepper

DIRECTIONS:

1. Please note: these recipes use sauerkraut and Dulce seaweed. They are responsible for the process of fermentation of the product (in fact, why sauces have an unusual taste).
2. To "languish" sauces in a dehydrator, we will use clean, dried glass jars with tightly closed rubberized lids. Do not use plastic

or metal containers - this can ruin the taste and quality of the products.

3. To make the texture of sauces the most delicate and uniform, it is better to whip the ingredients in a powerful blender. But, in principle, a food processor with an S-shaped nozzle is also suitable - just then it will take a little longer to work with each sauce.

4. Alternately beat the ingredients for each sauce in a blender shift each sauce into a separate jar. Beat the first sauce, transfer it to the jar, and immediately wash the blender thoroughly. Only then we work with the second sauce. After the second sauce, also wash the blender.

5. We close the lids at the jars; put the jars in the dehydrator chamber. We set the temperature 35-40 ° C, the time - 16-20 hours and close the shutter.

6. So, when our smart dehydrator RawMid Dream Vitamin DDV-07 completes the work process, it immediately tells us about it - it beeps loudly. We go to the call and take out jars with a collection of wonderful ready-made sauces.

7. Such sauces should be stored in the refrigerator for up to 4 days, under tightly closed lids. These sauces are so delicious that they will not last longer!

NUTRITION: Calories: 370 Protein: 10.24 g Fat: 31.11 g Carbs: 18.27 g

74. Mocha Cake (Raw)

Preparation Time: 30 minutes

Cooking Time: 2 hours

Serving: 4

INGREDIENTS:

- 2.5 tbsp. Seedlings of buckwheat
- Cake from 1 medium squash and from 300 g apples
- 300 g dates
- 4 tbsp. l liquid coconut oil
- 1 slice of raw chocolate to decorate (optional)

DIRECTIONS:

1. Squeeze juice from zucchini and apples.
2. Delicious juice to drink with pleasure.
3. Squeeze punch in a submersible blender with 1.5 tbsp. buckwheat seedlings, distribute in a thin layer on dehydrator sheets and dry at a temperature not exceeding 45 ° C.

4. Rinse and soak the dates in clean cold water overnight - during this time the "dough" from the cake and buckwheat will just dry.

5. Remove the seeds out from the dates, place the dates in a blender, add 1 tbsp. buckwheat seedlings, coconut oil and "punch" to the most uniform consistency.

6. Break the dried "dough" into small pieces, place in a blender bowl with S-shaped knives and grind into crumbs.

7. Pour the crumbs into a deep bowl and, adding a little water, rubbing the mixture with your hand, to achieve the effect of wet crumbs. Like 10 photos in a cheesecake recipe (where the crimson dough is in blue).

8. Add a cream of dates, seedlings and coconut oil to wet crumbs. Mix. Put in a suitable shape.

NUTRITION: Calories: 339 Protein: 2.07 g Fat: 13.94 g Carbs: 57.75 g

75. Nutless Cheesecake (Raw)

Preparation Time: 30 minutes

Cooking Time: 2 hours

Serving: 4

INGREDIENTS:

- 2.5 tbsp. green buckwheat
- 500 g carrots, beets
- 5-7 Art. 1 maple syrup or agave syrup
- 1 lemon
- 4-5 Art. (Melted cocoa butter)

DIRECTIONS:

1. In the morning, thoroughly rinse the green buckwheat; soak it in clean cold water. In the evening, thoroughly rinse the buckwheat under running water; leave it without water for the night.
2. In the morning, seedlings will already appear.
3. Peel the necessary amount of carrots and beets, squeeze the juice.

4. Therefore the dough turned out very pink. If you take beets less, the dough will be browner. If you use only carrots - orange. Although the red dough also looks amazing! So choose to your taste how many beets or carrots to take for your cake.

5. And yes, do not forget about squeezed juice: a mixture of carrot and beetroot juice is super-healthy; do not deprive yourself of the opportunity to enjoy it!

6. Squeeze the juice into a deep bowl.

7. Add half the buckwheat seedlings, zest, 1/3 lemon juice and 2-3 tbsp. l syrup.

8. Rinse the remaining buckwheat seedlings under running water. Leave them without water for further germination.

9. Using a submersible blender, grind everything thoroughly to a state of uniform dense mass.

10. We taste the mixture. We should get a tasty, moderately sweet dough with a distinct lemon flavor.

11. Now add the zest or syrup - as you wish. But do not overdo it, because when the product dries, the taste becomes more saturated.

12. As thin as possible, distribute all the dough on elastic sheets of the dehydrator. It is not necessary to level the surface - we will still grind cooked cakes, as they say, into dust.

13. The dough from the specified number of ingredients took 2.5 sheets.

14. Put the sheets to dry in a dehydrator until completely dry - at a temperature of no higher than 45 ° C.

15. Look here: if you cook the dough in the morning and apply it to the sheets with a sufficiently thin layer, it should certainly dry by the evening.

16. Remove dried cakes from sheets.

17. Break the crusts into pieces, place in the bowl of the combined blender with S-shaped knives.

18. Grind the pieces until small crumbs, and then pour into a deep cup.

19. Add a little water to the crumb, mix.

20. By the way, dry crumbs cannot be used all at once. If you are going to cook a cake of a small form (or the cake mold itself is small), then moisten the required amount of crumbs. Use the rest next time.

21. At the bottom of the cake mold, put the dough in a layer about 1 cm high, carefully compact

22. Grind cocoa butter, melt.

23. Buckwheat seedlings left in the morning, rinse thoroughly under running water. Put them in a glass of a hand blender. Add 1/3 lemon juice, melted cocoa butter, syrup. Punch the mixture to the most uniform consistency.

24. Taste the mixture. Add sourness (due to lemon juice) or sweets (due to syrup) - in general, do as you like.

25. If you think the cream is too watery, add some more cocoa butter. But you should not get too carried away with oil.

26. Pour the mixture into the mold on the dough; put the cake in the refrigerator. Top of the cake can be sprinkled with the remaining

crumbs. Then a piece of the finished cake can be served without any additional decoration.

27. And you can fill the top of the cake with live jam - for example, from raspberries or viburnum. In any case, decorate your cake as your imagination suggests.

28. In the title photo, my cake (I served it for the New Year) is decorated with viburnum syrup on top.

29. Such a cheesecake can be stored in the freezer for up to 4-5 days.

NUTRITION: Calories: 74 Protein: 1.43 g Fat: 1.5 g Carbs: 15.12 g

Chapter 13: Side Dishes

76. Zucchini Chips

Preparation time: 15 minutes

Cooking time: 12 hours

Servings: 8

INGREDIENTS:

- 4 cups zucchini, sliced thinly
- 2 tbsp. balsamic vinegar
- 2 tbsp. olive oil
- 2 tsp. sea salt

DIRECTION:

1. Add olive oil, balsamic vinegar, and sea salt to the large bowl and stir well.
2. Add sliced zucchini to the bowl and toss well.
3. Arrange zucchini slices on dehydrator trays and dehydrate at 135 F/ 58 C for 8-12 hours.
4. Store in air-tight container.

NUTRITION: Calories: 40 Fat: 3.6g Protein: 0.7g Carbs: 1.9g

77. Eggplant Slices

Preparation time: 10 minutes

Cooking time: 4 hours

Servings: 4

INGREDIENTS:

- 1 medium eggplant, cut into ¼ inch thick slices
- ¼ tsp. onion powder
- ¼ tsp. garlic powder
- 1 ½ tsp. paprika

DIRECTIONS:

1. Add all ingredients into the mixing bowl and toss well.
2. Arrange eggplant slices on dehydrator trays and dehydrate at 145 F/ 63 C for 4 hours or until crispy.
3. Store in air-tight container.

NUTRITION: Calories: 32 Fat: 0.3g Protein: 1.3g Carbs: 7.4g

78. Tasty Zucchini Chips

Preparation time: 15 minutes

Cooking time: 8 hours

Servings: 4

INGREDIENTS:

- 2 medium zucchini wash and cut into ¼ inch slices
- 1/8 tsp. cayenne pepper
- ½ tsp. garlic powder
- 1 tsp. olive oil
- 1/8 tsp. sea salt

DIRECTION:

1. Add all ingredients into the mixing bowl and toss well to coat.
2. Arrange zucchini slices on dehydrator trays and dehydrate at 135 F/ 58 C for 6-8 hours.
3. Store in air-tight container.

NUTRITION: Calories: 27 Fat: 1.4g Protein: 1.3g Carbs: 3.6g

79. Brussels Sprout Chips

Preparation time: 15 minutes

Cooking time: 10 hours

Servings: 6

INGREDIENTS:

- 2 lbs. Brussels sprouts, wash, dry, cut the root and separate leaves
- 2 fresh lemon juice
- ½ cup water
- ¼ cup nutritional yeast
- 1 jalapeno pepper halved and remove seeds
- 1 cup cashews
- 2 bell peppers
- 1 tsp. sea salt

DIRECTIONS:

1. Add Brussels sprouts leaves to the large bowl and set aside.
2. Add bell peppers, water, lemon juice, nutritional yeast, jalapeno, cashews, and salt to the blender and blend until smooth.
3. Pour blended mixture over Brussels sprouts leaves and toss until well coated.
4. Arrange Brussels sprouts on dehydrator trays and dehydrate at 125 F/ 52 C for 10 hours.
5. Allow to cool completely then store in air-tight container.

NUTRITION: Calories: 237 Fat: 11.7g Protein: 12.3g Carbs: 27.7g

80. Kale Chips

Preparation time: 10 minutes

Cooking time: 4 hours

Servings: 4

INGREDIENTS:

- 2 kale heads
- 1 tsp. garlic powder
- 1 tsp. sea salt
- 1 tbsp. fresh lemon juice
- 3 tbsp. nutritional yeast
- 2 tbsp. olive oil

DIRECTIONS:

1. Wash kale and cut into bits.
2. Add remaining ingredients into the bowl and mix well.
3. Add kale bits to the bowl and mix until well coated.
4. Arrange kale bits on dehydrator trays and dehydrate at 145 F/ 63 C for 3-4 hours or until crispy.

NUTRITION: Calories: 111 Fat: 7.5g Protein: 4.9g Carbs: 8.5g

81. Dried Bell Peppers

Preparation time: 10 minutes

Cooking time: 24 hours

Servings: 4

INGREDIENTS:

- 4 bell peppers cut in half and de-seed

DIRECTIONS:

1. Cut bell peppers in strips then cut each strip in ½ inch pieces.
2. Arrange bell peppers strips on dehydrator racks and dehydrate at 135 F/ 58 C for 12-24 hours or until crisp.
3. Store in air-tight container.

NUTRITION: Calories: 38 Fat: 0.3g Protein: 1.2g Carbs: 9g

82. Avocado Chips

Preparation time: 15 minutes

Cooking time: 10 hours

Servings: 4

INGREDIENTS:

- 4 avocados, halved and pitted
- ¼ tsp. sea salt
- ¼ tsp. cayenne pepper
- ¼ cup fresh cilantro, chopped
- ½ lemon juice

DIRECTIONS:

1. Cut avocado into the slices.
2. Drizzle lemon juice over avocado slices.
3. Arrange avocado slices on dehydrator trays and sprinkle with cayenne pepper, salt and cilantro dehydrate at 160 F/ 71 C for 10 hours.

NUTRITION: Calories: 62 Fat: 5.1g Protein: 1.1g Carbs: 3.2g

83. Sweet Potato Chips

Preparation time: 10 minutes

Cooking time: 12 hours

Servings: 2

INGREDIENTS:

- 2 sweet potatoes peel and sliced thinly
- 1/8 tsp. ground cinnamon
- 1 tsp. coconut oil, melted
- Seal salt

DIRECTIONS:

1. Add sweet potato slices in a bowl. Add cinnamon, coconut oil, and salt and toss well.
2. Arrange sweet potato slices on dehydrator trays and dehydrate at 125 F/ 52 C for 12 hours.
3. Store in air-tight container.

NUTRITION: Calories: 132 Fat: 2.3g Protein: 2.1g Carbs: 26.3g

84. Healthy Squash Chips

Preparation time: 10 minutes

Cooking time: 12 hours

Servings: 8

INGREDIENTS:

- 1 yellow squash, cut into 1/8 inch thick slices
- 2 tbsp. apple cider vinegar
- 2 tsp. olive oil
- Salt

DIRECTIONS:

1. Add all ingredients into the bowl and toss well.
2. Arrange squash slices on dehydrator trays and dehydrate at 115 F/ 46 C for 12 hours or until crispy.
3. Store in air-tight container.

NUTRITION: Calories: 15 Fat: 1.2g Protein: 0.3g Carbs: 0.9g

85. Broccoli Chips

Preparation time: 15 minutes

Cooking time: 12 hours

Servings: 4

INGREDIENTS:

- 1 lb. broccoli, cut into florets
- 1 tsp. onion powder
- 1 garlic clove
- ½ cup vegetable broth
- ¼ cup hemp seeds
- 2 tbsp. nutritional yeast

DIRECTIONS:

1. Add broccoli florets in a large mixing bowl and set aside.
2. Add remaining ingredients into the blender and blend until smooth.
3. Pour blended mixture over broccoli florets and toss well.
4. Arrange broccoli florets on dehydrator trays and dehydrate at 115 F/ 46 C for 10-12 hours.

NUTRITION: Calories: 106 Fat: 4.3g Protein: 8.7g Carbs: 11.2g

Chapter 14: Soups

86. Chicken Noodle Soup

Preparation time: 10 minutes

Cooking time: 25 minutes

Servings: 4

INGREDIENTS:

- ¼ cup red lentils
- 1 bay leaf
- 1 cup egg noodles
- 1/8 tsp. celery seed
- 1/8 tsp. garlic powder
- ½ tsp. dill seed
- 1 ½ tbsp. chicken bouillon granules
- 2 tbsp. dehydrated sliced onion
- 8 cups water

DIRECTIONS:

1. Add all ingredients except water into the glass jar. Seal jar with lid tightly and shake well.
2. To cook: Add water and jar content to the saucepan and bring to boil.
3. Reduce heat and simmer for 25 minutes.
4. Serve and enjoy.

NUTRITION: Calories: 108 Fat: 1.1g Protein: 5.2g Carbs: 19.6g

87. Minestrone Soup

Preparation time: 10 minutes

Cooking time: 12 minutes

Servings: 4

INGREDIENTS:

- ¼ cup dehydrated corn
- ¼ cup dehydrated bell peppers
- ¼ cup dehydrated carrots
- ¼ cup dehydrated peas
- ¼ cup dehydrated green beans
- ¼ cup dehydrated sliced onion
- ¼ cup dehydrated celery
- ¾ cup pasta
- 1 tbsp. dried beef bouillon
- 1 tsp. dried parsley
- ½ tsp. Italian seasoning
- ¼ cup tomato powder
- 6 cups water

DIRECTIONS:

1. Add all ingredients except water into the glass jar. Seal jar tightly with lid and shake well.
2. To cook: Add water and jar content to the saucepan and bring to boil.
3. Reduce heat and simmer for 12 minutes or until vegetable and pasta are cooked.
4. Serve and enjoy.

NUTRITION: Calories: 128 Fat: 1g Protein: 3.6g Carbs: 28.1g

88. Chicken Tortilla Soup

Preparation time: 10 minutes

Cooking time: 30 minutes

Servings: 6

INGREDIENTS:

- 1 cup dehydrated chicken
- ¼ tsp. ground chipotle pepper
- 1 cup dried corn
- 2/3 cup dried green chilies
- ½ cup dehydrated sliced onion
- 1 tsp. garlic powder
- 2 tsp. chicken bouillon
- 1 ½ tbsp. chili powder
- ½ cup tomato powder
- 8 cups water

DIRECTIONS:

1. Add all ingredients into the glass jar. Seal jar tightly with lid and shake well.
2. To cook: Add water and jar content to the saucepan and bring to boil.
3. Reduce heat and simmer for 15-20 minutes.
4. Serve with tortilla chips.

NUTRITION: Calories: 120 Fat: 1.6g Protein: 9.8g Carbs: 19.2g

89. Beef Bell Pepper Soup

Preparation time: 15 minutes

Cooking time: 30 minutes

Servings: 6

INGREDIENTS:

- ½ cup freeze-dried ground beef
- ¾ cup instant brown rice
- ¼ cup dried celery
- 1/3 cup dehydrated sliced onion
- 1 cup dehydrated bell peppers
- 1 tbsp. beef bouillon
- 1 tsp. garlic powder
- ¾ cup tomato powder
- ¼ cup freeze dried sausage crumbled
- 9 cups water

DIRECTIONS:

1. Add all ingredients except water into the glass jar. Seal jar tightly with lid.
2. To cook: Add water and jar content to the saucepan and bring to boil.
3. Reduce heat and simmer for 15-20 minutes.
4. Serve and enjoy.

NUTRITION: Calories: 171 Fat: 2.3g Protein: 6.9g Carbs: 32.3g

90. Vegetable Soup

Preparation time: 15 minutes

Cooking time: 30 minutes

Servings: 6

INGREDIENTS:

- 1/3 cup dried vegetable flakes (any combination of tomatoes, peas, onions, broccoli, zucchini, celery, carrots)
- ¼ teaspoon dried parsley
- ¼ teaspoon dried sweet basil
- Pinch garlic powder
- Pinch onion powder
- 1 tablespoon bulgar wheat
- 1 teaspoon pasta, broken if large pieces
- 2 cups chicken or beef

DIRECTIONS:

1. Place vegetable flakes, parsley, basil, garlic powder, onion powder, bulgar wheat, and pasta in a pint thermos. Bring broth or stock to a rolling boil and pour over dry Ingredients. Cover thermos and close securely for 10-15 minutes. Add salt and pepper to taste.

NUTRITION: Calories: Fat: 2.3g Protein: 6.9g Carbs: 32.3g

91. Spinach Soup with Avocado and Herbs (Raw)

Preparation time: 15 minutes

Cooking/Dry time: 4 hours

Serving: 3-4

INGREDIENTS:

- 1 soft avocado
- 60 g of spinach
- 2 g of garlic (4 small cloves or arrows of garlic greens)
- 900 ml of water (can be warm)
- Ground black pepper to taste
- 1/2 tbsp. l lemon juice
- "Garnish":
- 50 g zucchini
- 40 g cilantro
- 30 g dill
- 20 g borage leaves (cucumber grass)
- 10 g beet leaves
- 50 g white or green onions
- Supplement:

- Radish
- pink tomato
- champignons
- lemon juice
- honey
- favorite spices
- seaweed Dulce

DIRECTIONS:

1. Beat all products for the base of the broth in a blender until a smooth, homogeneous mass.

2. Grate zucchini with straws. Finely chop all the greens.

3. Pour zucchini and greens into the tureen; pour the base for the broth.

4. Serve separately chopped radish and pink tomato for the soup.

5. Very good if you add dried mushrooms and Dulce seaweed

6. To the soup. To do this, cut mushrooms into thin slices; pickle them for 1 hour in a marinade of lemon juice, honey and spices.

7. Then for 4 hours, dry the mushrooms in a dehydrator.

8. Algae must be soaked and finely chopped before being added.

9. The most important thing in this soup is the tender base.

10. Spinach and garlic should not be much; otherwise a fairly noticeable bitterness will be present in the dish;

11. A large number of various greens certainly plays an important role here - the more diverse, the brighter the aroma!

12. And if you do not add onions and garlic here, then such a soup can easily be taken with you to work.

NUTRITION: Calories: 128 Protein: 3.62 g Fat: 6.9 g Carbs: 14.43 g

Chapter 15: Snacks

92. Muesli Home Made

Preparation time: 15 minutes

Cooking/Dry time: 4 hours

Serving: 3-4

INGREDIENTS:

- 1/8 cup flakes with three cereals (brown wheat rice barley)
- 1 cup oatmeal
- 2/3 cup puffed rice
- ¼ cup honey-blown kamut
- 1 tbsp. coconut flour
- 1 golden apple
- 2 bananas
- 4 slices fresh pineapple

DIRECTIONS:

1. Cut the sliced bananas, apple and pineapple into cubes. Spread the fruit in the basket and start at 113 degrees. When all the fruit is completely dried, mix the Ingredients and store in a lid container. You can also add dried strawberries. They will give a unique flavor to your Muesli but should be used in moderation precisely because once dried they are a real concentrated taste and sweetness; you will find that very few slices are enough.

NUTRITION: Calories: 405 Protein: 6.45 g Fat: 5.76 g Carbs: 95.29 g

93. Apple Chips

Preparation time: 15 minutes

Cooking/Dry time: 16 hours

Serving: 3-4

INGREDIENTS:

- Apples
- Lemon
- 1 cinnamon stick (optional)

DIRECTIONS:

1. Wash the apples and slice them with a thickness of about 1/3 inch so as not to blacken them, put them in a bowl with water and lemon juice. The peel contains many vitamins, do not throw them away! Place the apples on a clean cloth and dry them well, then place them in the dryer baskets and start at 104-122 degrees F for 12-16 hours then at 149 degrees F for an hour if you want to get the crisp effect of chips. Let them cool and then close them in an airtight container or tin box. If you love the scent of cinnamon add a stick.

NUTRITION: Calories: 27 Protein: 0.17 g Fat: 0.11 g Carbs: 7.31 g

94. Apple & Chocolate Chips

Preparation time: 15 minutes

Cooking/Dry time: 20 hours

Serving: 3-4

INGREDIENTS:

- Apples
- dark chocolate

DIRECTIONS:

1. Thoroughly wash the apples and remove them from the core without dividing them. Cut into slices about 4-5 mm thick and place them in the dryer at 122 degrees F. Apples take between 12 and 20 hours to dry out completely. Melt the dark chocolate in Bain-marie (or in the microwave on low) stirring so that no lumps are forming, then dip the apple slices 1st 1 only until halfway. Put the Chocolates to cool and solidify on a wire rack (arrange them gently so as not to make it paste). Once dried - after about an hour - the chocolates are ready. Store them in airtight bags or glass jars.

NUTRITION: Calories: 25 Protein: 0.14 g Fat: 0.18 g Carbs: 6.4 g

95. Fruit Lollipops

Preparation time: 15 minutes

Cooking/Dry time: 15 hours

Serving: 3-4

INGREDIENTS:

- kiwi, bananas, apples
- 1 tbsp. caster sugar juice
- Water
- lemon juice

DIRECTIONS:

1. Peel and cut the fruit into slices of about 5 mm then put them in the dryer at 235 degrees F until completely dehydrated. On a sheet of parchment paper lay the dried slices slightly sticking the toothpick into the pulp and pour over the dissolved sugar with water and lemon. Let it solidify for 15 minutes then put the lollipops in the dryer at 113 degrees F for an hour.

NUTRITION: Calories: 11 Protein: 0.04 g Fat: 0.03g Carbs: 2.85 g

96. Fresh Fruit Bar

Preparation time: 15 minutes

Cooking/Dry time: 40 hours

Serving: 3-4

INGREDIENTS:

- previously dried fruit to taste
- Fresh apple
- flaxseeds
- sunflower seeds
- sesame seeds
- ground almonds
- oatmeal
- whole sugar

DIRECTIONS:

1. Combine the Ingredients by paying attention to the proportions: the mixture will have to consist of two-thirds of a mixture of dried fruit and for one third of the other dried foods in more or less equivalent quantities. There is no need to soak the flaxseeds because the fresh apple, which is grated to obtain a creamy pulp, binds the various Ingredients. It also rehydrates the dried fruit which becomes softer and is allowed to mix more easily. You will have a soft and malleable mixture but if it is too moist, add a few oatmeal.

2. Spread the dough on a sheet of baking paper and put it in the dryer at 140 degrees F for 40 hours by turning the bar a couple of times. However, the drying of the surface is a little slower and you have to be careful when overturning it the first time.

NUTRITION: Calories: 31 Protein: 0.34 g Fat: 0.62 g Carbs: 6.79 g

97. Raw Vegetable Burgers / Cutlets

Preparation time: 15 minutes

Cooking/Dry time: 4 hours

Serving: 3-4

INGREDIENTS:

- 1 1/2 cups pumpkin seeds (pre-soaked for several hours)
- 3 large carrots
- 1 medium onion
- Small bunch of parsley
- Juice of one lime or small lemon
- 1 clove of garlic
- Salt to taste
- 1/2 tsp. cumin
- 1/2 tsp. curry

DIRECTIONS:

1. Cut the carrots into pieces, put together with the rest of the ingredients in a combine with an S-shaped knife. Grind to a homogeneous consistency, but not to a puree state. Small pieces should be visible.

2. So, we have minced vegetables.

3. With wet hands, carefully sculpt small patties or small burgers.

4. In fact, these cutlets are already edible.

5. Such forcemeat can be used as a vegetable paste, but it will be most delicious if the cutlets are slightly dried to brown.

6. Put on pallets in a dehydrator, Set at 40-45 ° C.

7. After 2-3 hours, the patties are lightly browned. Then turn them over and hold for another 1 hour or a little longer - depending on how much dried cutlets you prefer.

8. Garnish with greens and eat with any juicy fresh salad and sauce / ketchup.

NUTRITION: Calories: 293 Protein: 14.19 g Fat: 21.97 g Carbs: 15.7 g

Chapter 16: Are Nutrients Lost During Drying?

There are some nutrients lost during pretreatment and drying. Any time the food is exposed to heat, light or oxygen, there will be some degradation of nutritional value. The longer the exposure, the greater the damage. Most fruits start degrading as soon as they're harvested. This degradation is sped up by cutting into them or otherwise exposing the flesh to oxygen.

Many fruits contain enzymes that react to the air and cause browning and nutrient loss to begin as soon as they're cut into. If you've ever left an apple or a banana out for a while and seen it turn brown, you've seen these enzymes in action. This reaction to the oxygen in the air can be slowed to a crawl by pretreating or blanching the fruit after it's been cut. The following vitamins can be damaged by too much heat, light or air exposure:

- Folate (heat).
- Riboflavin (heat).

- Thiamine (heat, light).
- Vitamin A (air, light).
- Vitamin B12 (heat, light).
- Vitamin C (air, heat).
- Vitamin E (air, heat, light).
- Vitamin K (light).
- Vitamin B6 (air).

Commercial foods that undergo intense treatment lose a lot more nutrients than fruit dried at home. While commercially dried foods can lose up to 80% of certain vitamins, foods dried at home usually don't come anywhere near that magnitude.

Take the following precautions to reduce the amount of vitamins lost while treating and drying produce:

Work on small batches of food at a time.

When you work on large batches and try to get a lot of fruit done at once, the pieces you cut into first are left to sit out while you process the rest of the produce. This can result in the earlier pieces degrading a lot faster than those cut later on.

Move food into pretreatment shortly after it's been cut.

Time is of essence when treating fruit that's prone to discoloration. It's important to slow down enzymatic reactions as early as possible to avoid nutrient loss.

Carefully regulate heat.

High heat can accelerate nutrient loss, so its important heat is monitored closely. Using a dehydrator allows you the most control over the amount of heat drying food is exposed to. Blanching also exposes food to heat and can damage nutrients, but may be critical to ensuring food can be properly stored. Blanching isn't as critical of a process with fruit as it is with vegetables.

Store dried food in an airtight container.

This will minimize the amount of air the food comes in contact with. If air is allowed into the container, the food can take up moisture from the air, drastically shortening how long the food will last.

Drying food in the sun exposes it to UV rays that can damage light-sensitive vitamins.

When vitamin retention is of concern, a dehydrator may be the better choice for drying.

Store food in small, single-serving containers.

Every time you open a container, more air is let in. Using single serving containers only exposes the food you plan on eating to new air.

No minerals are lost during the drying process, but pretreatment can cause some mineral loss. Boiling or otherwise exposing fruit to water may cause some of the minerals to leach out into the water. This can happen during blanching and again during rehydration. The drying process itself doesn't affect minerals.

Calories and sugar are largely unaffected by the drying process, but they will be concentrated into a smaller package. A raisin has the same caloric content and amount of sugar as it did when it was a grape, but it's now packed into the smaller raisin. Dried produce has more calories and more sugar than regular produce when compared by volume. For example, 100 grams of grapes have 15 grams of sugar and 70 calories. 100 grams of raisins have 60 grams of sugar and 300 calories. Raisins have 3 times the sugar and more than 4 times the calories than grapes when compared by volume.

For this reason, it's important not to overeat when it comes to dried fruit and vegetables. They can be a healthy part of most diets, but only if consumed in moderation.

Chapter 17: Why should I Dehydrate Food?

In the past, people dehydrated food because they didn't know when they would fresh stuff again. They also needed easy-to-carry food because of frequent traveling. Now, this doesn't describe most of our lives, so why would you need to ever dehydrate? There are still good reasons:

Saves money

Saving money is arguably the top reason to dehydrate. If you buy a bunch of produce and know you can't use it all before it goes bad, dehydrate them. This is a really great idea with herbs, since people rarely use very much at a time, and the herbs end up rotting. You can also save money by never needing to buy out-of-season produce when you're craving it. You can buy fresh when it's in season, dehydrate it, and eat it when the stuff at the store shoots up in price. By dehydrating your own snacks, you're also saving money by not buying packaged stuff, which is prohibitively expensive for a lot of people.

Saves space

Saving space is another reason to start dehydrating. Removing moisture from food dramatically shrinks it, so you can now fit 20+ pounds of dried food easily in a cupboard. For maximum space-saving, using freezer bags is better than glass jars or containers, because you can lay them flat. They can also be vacuum-sealed and shrink even further. For small kitchens and pantries, storage won't be a problem anymore when you dehydrate what you can.

Taste (and nutrition)

Dehydrated foods often taste better than when they're fresh, because their flavors are intensified. Moisture literally "waters down" flavor, so dried fruits taste much sweeter, even without added sugar. Dehydrated mushrooms are so flavorful that many chefs use them as a spice, not a vegetable, while a small handful of sun-dried tomato flavors an entire pasta dish. The icing on the cake is that dehydrated food also maintains their nutritional value. Removing the moisture doesn't destroy healthy vitamins, minerals, or calories.

Clean-eating

You can buy dried fruits, vegetables, and other snacks at the store, but more often than not, they're full of sugar and artificial ingredients. Even though dried foods last longer than fresh ones, packaged versions usually contain preservatives to make them last even longer. This is especially true for dried meats, which are not only highly-processed, they're usually extremely salty. Processed meat has also been classified as carcinogenic, which means it contains chemicals that might cause certain types of cancer! For all of this, you also pay a pretty penny. Making your own dehydrated snacks at home means you have total control over what goes in and what stays out.

Easy to carry around

There aren't a lot of truly portable snacks and the ones that are, like fruits and vegetables, got easily squished and bruised. When they're dry, they're hardened and much more durable. They also don't take up much space in a bag and they don't squirt juice everywhere when you're trying to eat them. Dehydrated food is the way to go if you're always on the run.

Dehydrating food at home saves money and space, makes clean and tasty snacks, and reduces food waste.

Reduces waste

We throw away a ton of food. In the US, we waste over $160 billion in food every year. While a lot of that comes from restaurants and grocery stores, the average person wastes a lot of the food they buy. It's basically like throwing away money. By dehydrating foods that don't stay fresh for very long, you're doing your part to reduce waste and get the most bang for your buck.

.

Conclusion

There are a number of structural changes food undergoes during the dehydration process. As heat or energy is applied to the food, water migrates out and evaporated. The larger the food is and the more water it contains, the harder it becomes to dry. For this reason, an entire watermelon is much more difficult to dry than a grape. Watermelon can be dried, but it needs to be cut into manageable pieces that'll dry all the way through before the inside starts to go bad while the outside dried.

This applies to pretty much any food you can imagine. Small tomatoes can be cut in half to dry. Larger tomatoes need to be sliced into thin slices to give them the best chance to dry. You'll never get an entire squash or a whole potato dry before they go bad, but chop them up and you have a completely different story.

Properly dried foods will contain a fraction of the liquid they once had. Some foods lose as much as 98% of their moisture during the drying process. For fruits and vegetables, the percentage is usually closer to 95%. Because most foods contain large amounts of moisture, drastic loss of volume comes about as a result of drying, with some foods shrinking down to less than a third of their original size.

Dried food is typically brittle and can be snapped in half when bent. If food is still moist and pliable after drying, it should be returned to the dryer.

As moisture leaves food, it often shrivels up and takes on a leathery, tough texture. The skin will wrinkle as the food inside shrinks. Compare a raisin to a grape taken straight off the vine and you get the picture.

Conclusion

Grapes lose a lot of volume as the moisture inside them evaporates and they become raisins.

The shrinkage in volume results in everything inside being concentrated into a smaller package. The caloric content doesn't change, which results in food that packs significantly more calories into each ounce than fresh food of the same variety. The vitamins and minerals that aren't lost to the drying process are all concentrated as well.

Dehydrated foods do lose some of their nutritional value, as vitamins like vitamin C; thiamin and vitamin B2 can be lost during drying and treating foods to prepare them for drying. Most studies of nutrient losses in dried foods are done on commercially-dried foods that undergo harsh treatment during the drying process. High heat and chemicals destroy much of the nutritional value. Most manufacturers aren't as concerned with creating nutritional foods as they are with putting out high volume. Most people don't know or care about vitamin loss. If it looks and tastes like dried food and can be bought at a reasonable price, they're happy.

In addition to lost nutrients, chemical reactions can occur once the food has been cut into and the color, texture and taste of the food can be impacted. Food that's been dried and rehydrated is rarely exactly the same as fresh food. It's close enough that it can be used in culinary dishes that call for it, but it probably isn't going to be close enough for you to want to eat it on its own. I love celery and peanut butter, but there isn't much to love about reconstituted celery and peanut butter. Take the same dried celery and put it in a casserole or a soup and no one will never know the difference. Dried foods will never completely replace fresh foods, but they can be used as a convenient and easy addition to a number of food items to which you'd like to add nutritional value.

Browning reactions are one of the most common chemical reactions that occur in dried foods. They occur when chemical compounds in the food being dried react with compounds in the air. Browning is usually considered undesirable because it can change the taste of the food as it changes its appearance. A little known fact about browning is it can sometimes damage the nutritional value of the food as the color changes. Many fruits and vegetables undergo enzymatic browning when they're cut open and their flesh is exposed to the air. This sort of browning also occurs when produce is dropped, hit with something or otherwise damaged. It's a stress response brought on by the rapid conversion of chemical compounds in the flesh into brown melanin. The enzymes that cause browning can be deactivated through careful use of heat, acids or chemicals like sulphites. Blanching foods and/or exposing them to citric acids before setting them out to dry can inhibit browning enough to where it isn't much of a problem.

When a recipe calls for blanching fruit or vegetables, it's usually done to stop or slow enzymatic action on the produce. Foods that need blanching should be processed quickly after cutting into them. The enzymatic action will initiate as soon as the flesh of the fruit or vegetable is exposed to oxygen. If you're planning on drying large amounts of produce, it's best to do so in smaller batches. Trying to do it all in one batch might result in the produce you cut in the beginning degrading to the point it can't be used by the time you get around to blanching it.

Color loss can also come about as a result of drying. This effect is especially pronounced when high heat or sunlight is used to dry leafy greens and brightly-colored vegetables that get their color from carotenoids, which are fat-soluble pigments. Pigments will often fade during drying and can further fade during storage.

Dried foods change texture when the moisture is removed. This is due to a number of factors, including the loss of moisture, changes to the cellulose material and degradation of some of the compounds found in the food. When foods are dried at too high a temperature, the outside of the food can dry before all the moisture leaves the inside, creating what's known as case-hardened foods. They appear dry on the outside, but there's still too much moisture inside the hard outer shell.

While it may sound like food drying is an invasive process that drastically changes food, it actually isn't that bad once you get past the physical changes. It's the least damaging food preservation technique and foods that are dried retain most of their nutritional value. Other preservation techniques involve the use of extreme heat or extreme cold, which is even more damaging to the structure and chemical composition of foods subjected to them.

From a technical standpoint, most food starts degrading as soon as it is harvested. Once a plant or animal is no longer alive, it starts to lose nutritional value. This loss is slow at first, but quickly accelerates into rapid degeneration once the food begins to spoil. Anything done to prepare the food like heating it, washing it, slicing it or otherwise processing it further damages the food.

Regardless of how fresh your food is when you start drying it, some nutrients are going to be lost during drying. Just how much and which nutrients are lost largely depends on the drying method used and whether the food is treated or processed before drying. Commercially dried foods can lose as much as 80% of their vitamin C and up to 20% of vitamin A.

Gently drying foods at home can help mitigate some of these losses, but won't completely eliminate lost nutrients. Taking steps to minimize the amount of heat and light dried foods are exposed to will help minimize the amount of vitamins lost as a result of exposure.

The following vitamins can be lost when food is exposed to too much heat:

- Folate.
- Riboflavin.
- Thiamine.
- Vitamin B12.
- Vitamin C.
- Vitamin E.

Sun drying can expose foods to high heats if drying is done in direct sunlight on a warm day. Drying indoors may be preferable when loss of nutrients is a concern. Drying in an oven with the temperature set too high can also expose food to a lot more heat than is necessary. Using a dehydrator allows for the most control over the amount of heat used during drying.

Air exposure damages the following vitamins:

- Vitamin A.
- Vitamin B6.
- Vitamin C.
- Vitamin E.

Conclusion

Air exposure is a little trickier to mitigate. Food has to be exposed to air during the drying process because the moisture leaving the food has to evaporate into the air. The best way to minimize air exposure is to ensure there is good circulation and to use a drying technique that dries food quickly, as opposed to leaving it sit for extended periods of time.

The following vitamins are sensitive to UV rays and can be damaged by exposure to direct sunlight:

- Thiamine.
- Vitamin A.
- Vitamin B6.
- Vitamin B12.
- Vitamin C.
- Vitamin E.
- Vitamin K.

Light exposure can be minimized by using methods of drying that don't expose the food to direct sunlight. For obvious reasons, sun drying is the worst offender when it comes to sunlight exposure.

Exposing certain foods like fruit to sulfur during the drying process can help save some of the vitamin A and C, but will destroy thiamine. It can also help slow enzymatic reactions, but there are some dangers associated with sulfuring.

No minerals, fiber or calories are lost during the drying process. If the food is soaked in brine prior to drying, some minerals may leach out into the water. Calories will remain the same in that one piece of fruit will have the same caloric content whether it's dried or not. The caloric count by volume will be much higher in dried fruit because the same amount of calories is packed into a smaller, lighter piece of fruit.

To illustrate this point, let's look at the caloric value of apples. A pound of raw apples has 240 calories. A pound of dried apples has around 1,500 calories. That's a huge difference in calories between dried and raw apples that are the same weight.

Be careful not to overeat when consuming dried foods, because a little food goes a long way, regardless of the nutritional losses due to processing and drying the food. When it comes to nutritional value, fresh food is almost always more nutritious than dried food. For foods dried at home using proper drying procedures, the loss is minimal and isn't of much concern. I hope you have learned something!

Printed in Great Britain
by Amazon

67107844R00173